"This book is a marvelous balance of sound theology and wise practical counsel for couples preparing for marriage. Rob Green writes as one who has faithfully shepherded men and women through this delightful process for many years. You will not only fall deeper in love with each other, but deeper in love with Jesus."

Steve Viars, Senior Pastor, Faith Church, Lafayette, IN

"Rob Green has given us a practical, biblical, *and* Jesus-focused premarital book to use with couples preparing for marriage. If marriage according to Ephesians 5:32 is really designed to put the love of Jesus and his bride (the church) on display, then it stands to reason that we should be talking about Jesus from the very beginning with couples who are preparing for marriage. Rob addresses all the critical areas that need to be covered but does it in a way that keeps coming back to Jesus. For years we've adapted existing material and always felt like something was missing. It wasn't something; it was *Someone,* and *Tying the Knot* puts that Someone back where he's supposed to be—at the center of marriage. There's no better way to help a couple get started right in marriage than to help them see Jesus at the center of it all."

Brad Bigney, Pastor, Grace Fellowship Church, Florence, KY; ACBC certified counselor; conference speaker; author of *Gospel Treason*

"Even if you never got farther than chapter 1 ("Jesus Must Be the Center of Your Life") in *Tying the Knot,* this book would be well worth reading. But if you continue reading, you'll find treasure piled upon treasure. This book will strengthen not only those just starting out in marriage, but also those who have been married for decades. Read it and be encouraged."

Amy Baker, Ministry Resource Director, Faith Church, Lafayette, IN; author of *Picture Perfect*

"As you anticipate your wedding, one of life's biggest events, there's no greater gift than a wise friend to help guide you along the pathway of preparation and decision-making. Rob Green serves as your friend on this journey, assisting you to build a foundation for a strong and lasting marriage. In addition to his useful teaching, the practical exercises per chapter, and mentor appendix prove invaluable."

Kevin Carson, Pastor, Sonrise Baptist Church, Ozark, MO; Professor, Baptist Bible College and Theological Seminary, Springfield, MO

"*Tying the Knot* offers a compelling vision of how Jesus must be central to your life and marriage. Such a vision gives hope, brings relief, and most important, stirs your affections for Christ. Rob, a seasoned husband and pastor, applies timeless gospel truths to matters of the heart while offering practical biblical guidance for those approaching their wedding day and for those married for years. I wholeheartedly recommend *Tying the Knot*."

Robert K. Cheong, Pastor of Care, Sojourn Community Church, Louisville, KY

"Rob has masterfully woven together three crucial elements for marriage and marriage preparation. *Tying the Knot* is solidly biblical, immensely practical, and unapologetically Christ-centered. Christian couples, pastors, and lay leaders will be well served in making this book one of their go-to resources for marriage preparation, and the church will be well served by this book for generations to come."

Jack Delk, Pastor for Counseling – North Campus, Bethlehem Baptist Church, Minneapolis, MN

"No one on earth truly knows what you will face in marriage—not in the details at least. Endless are the possible joys and pains, the trials and circumstances, the sins and graces, the shifts and surprises, the people who will come and go. Everything will change. Preparing for this is a serious task. Rob Green offers a kind of preparation for marriage that does not center upon the ever-shifting circumstances of life, but upon the Lord Jesus Christ and upon his everlasting Word. *Tying the Knot* labors to orient you around the Person who will be there, who knows what will come, who is faithful and mighty, and who will give you manifold wisdom for the endless possibilities of marriage."

John Henderson, Associate Pastor, Del Ray Baptist, Alexandria, VA

"One of the most neglected areas of counseling in the life of the church has to be premarital counseling. Often seen as a perfunctory hurdle to jump through, premarital counseling can quickly become stale and mechanical. Rob Green has provided the church an excellent new resource for premarital counseling that is biblically-saturated, Christ-centered, and clearly written. From the discussion questions at the end of each chapter to the guide for mentors in the back, this book is a perfect blend of theology for real life."

Jonathan Holmes, Pastor of Counseling, Parkside Church, author of *The Company We Keep*

"I would have loved to read this book with my wife while we were engaged. So practical, so wise. Engaged couples, listen carefully to Rob Green."

Andy Naselli, Assistant Professor of New Testament and Biblical Theology, Bethlehem College & Seminary, Minneapolis, MN

"Rob Green has provided us with a wonderful new gospel-centered re-source to help engaged couples prepare for marriage. This book repeatedly emphasizes that marriage is founded upon God's love for us in Christ and is filled with personal examples and practical illustrations that come from years of faithful biblical counseling. One of the best qualities of *Tying the Knot* is its brevity. Rob covers the most important issues succinctly so that a busy engaged couple should have sufficient time to complete this study and the homework assignments in the months leading up to marriage. Another unique feature is that Rob has gone to extra effort (including an appendix) to make it easy for a mentor couple to work through this material with an engaged couple. I am sure that the Lord will use this book to bless many and I look forward to using it with many couples in the future."

Jim Newheiser, Executive Director, The Institute for Biblical Counseling and Discipleship (ICBD)

"Premarital counseling is needed now more than ever in our culture. The scourge of unhappy marriages and so-easy divorce has led many to believe that marriage is an institution that is no longer workable. *Tying the Knot* is a hope-filled, theologically sound, 'you can do marriage God's way and here's how' manual. Green's careful unpacking of key Scriptures coupled with practical application assignments makes this book a winner. It is intended as a premarital counseling manual, but it would also be helpful for small group study or a sermon-series primer. Get it and use it!"

Randy Patten, Founder, TEAM Focus Ministries; former Director of Training and Advancement, The Association of Certified Biblical Counselors

"There has long been a need for a solid premarital counseling curriculum that roots everything in Scripture, is realistic about the joys and challenges of marriage, and most importantly makes Christ central to everything. Rob Green's *Tying the Knot* accomplishes this, and offers much, much more."

Deepak Reju, Pastor of Biblical Counseling and Family Ministry, Capitol Hill Baptist Church, Washington, DC; author of *The Pastor and Counseling* and *On Guard*; President of the Board, Biblical Counseling Coalition

"Companies have start-up manuals that they require you to read and follow when beginning a new job. Yet when it comes to starting one of the most important human relationships—marriage—many do not seek or even know to seek guidance and preparation from above for what is ahead. Rob has contributed a tremendous resource for the caring of souls in the church where new marriage engagements are concerned. *Tying the Knot* is Christ-centered, biblically-based, and easy to comprehend. This book comprehensively addresses the key issues in beginning and growing a marriage and would be invaluable for anyone embarking on their marital journey. I highly recommend this to pastors, counselors, young couples, and even as a refresher for married couples."

Stuart W. Scott, Professor of Biblical Counseling, The Master's College

"Dr. Rob Green's succinct and timely resource, *Tying the Knot*, helps couples strengthen their relationships with each other and with Christ as they work with a mentor to align their goals for the future with the biblical wisdom found in God's Word. The well-planned discussion questions in each chapter, the outline of the book, and the very helpful 'Just for the Mentors' section are but three of the great aspects of this book that will be much appreciated by pastors and all those who conduct premarital counseling."

Mark E. Shaw, Pastor and Executive Director, Vision of Hope; author of *The Heart of Addiction* and *Addiction-Proof Parenting*

"In all the pressures and expectations of planning for marriage, it is easy for a Christian couple to lose direction by focusing on the demands of the immediate. Rob Green has written a wonderful tool that will take a couples through essential elements of building a Christ-centered relationship. What he describes in this book is invaluable for marriages that desire to not just survive but thrive with a proper Christ focus."

John D. Street, Chair, MABC Graduate Program, The Master's College & Seminary; President, Association of Certified Biblical Counselors

"How does God minister his grace through you to another one of his children in marriage? In a culture of self, where can one get guidance for a Savior-focused marriage? In *Tying The Knot*, Rob Green provides a biblical, Christ-centered, practical, hope-filled tool to assist individuals in learning how to partner with Christ to become instruments of his grace to their spouses."

A. Charles Ware, President of Crossroads Bible College; coauthor of *Just Don't Marry One* and *Christ-Centered Biblical Counseling*

"Marital love, problem solving, roles and expectations, communication, finances, community, intimacy—all the issues that every marriage faces—can be addressed with self as the center or with Jesus as the center. Whether you're a pastor, counselor, marriage mentor, premarital couple, or married couple, use *Tying the Knot* to join marriages to the cross. From now on, this is *the* book I will recommend for premarital and marital counseling."

Bob Kellemen, Author of *Gospel-Centered Counseling* and *Gospel Conversations*

"*Tying the Knot* is a great book for those considering marriage. The topics are highly relevant and the homework will help any counselor or couple to put these crucial lessons into practice. I gladly recommend this book to anyone involved in premarital counseling."

Garrett Higbee, Executive Director of Biblical Soul Care, Harvest Bible Chapel and of the Biblical Counseling Coalition

"*Tying the Knot* shows the connection between having an amazing Savior and things like communication or budgets. Where it can be easy to fall into mechanistic teaching, Rob Green draws the line from Christ's obedience and provision to our lives. I appreciated his focus on the community of Christ and its importance in marriage. I recommend this book to anyone who is doing premarital counseling."

Elyse Fitzpatrick, Author of *Counsel from the Cross*

"Dr. Green has provided a resource I didn't know I needed so badly. Green understands two things particularly well: the dynamics of how real people relate and how those dynamics reveal their constant need for Jesus Christ. The practical exercises that flow from these insights will make it easy on counselors helping couples to prepare for marriage."

Jeremy Pierre, Associate Professor of Biblical Counseling & Dean of Students, The Southern Baptist Theological Seminary

Tying the Knot

Tying the Knot

A Premarital Guide
to a Strong and Lasting Marriage

Rob Green

New
Growth
Press

www.newgrowthpress.com

New Growth Press, Greensboro, NC 27404
Copyright © 2016 by Rob Green

Cover Design: Faceout Books, faceoutstudio.com
Interior Design and Typesetting: Lisa Parnell, lparnell.com

ISBN 978-1-942572-59-6 (Print)
ISBN 978-1-942572-60-2 (eBook)

Library of Congress Cataloging-in-Publication Data
Green, Rob (Robert Eric)
  Tying the knot : a premarital guide to a strong and lasting marriage / Rob Green.
    pages cm
  ISBN 978-1-942572-59-6 (pbk.) —
  ISBN 978-1-942572-60-2 (ebook)
1. Marriage—Religious aspects—Christianity. I. Title.
  BV835.G725 2016
  248.8'44—dc23
                                                    2015029199
Printed in the United States of America

25 24 23 22 21 20 19 18   5 6 7 8 9

To my dear wife, Stephanie,

*of twenty-two years. Thank you for entering the adventure
of marriage with me. Jesus explains in Mark 12 that marriage
is not for heaven; it is for now. This means that the joys God
has designed for marriage help us to live for Jesus
in both the blessings, like Yosemite,
and the challenges, like the loss of the child we never met,
of life in a beautiful, broken, twisted world.
Thank you for the joyful adventures so far.
I am looking forward to the ones still to come.*

Contents

Acknowledgments

MY THANKS GOES to Faith Church, Lafayette, Indiana, whose training in counseling has greatly shaped the way I think about my own life and the lives of others. My service at Faith provides many opportunities to counsel married people and those planning to marry in the near future. That training and experience have shaped much of what is written here.

Introduction

CONGRATULATIONS ON YOUR upcoming marriage! As someone who has counseled many engaged couples—and a married man myself—I am very glad that you have chosen this book to help you prepare for the wonderful experience of marriage. The engagement period is an exciting but busy time; there's always something new to talk about and something new to plan. That's why I'm encouraged that you have chosen to invest time and energy in material that can help you to have a Christ-centered marriage. As you study this book—and more importantly, the Bible—you will prepare yourself to have a strong and lasting marriage.

This book is for couples who want premarital counseling that is Christ-centered. Why is this important? First, it's important because God designed marriage. Marriage was his idea. He designed marriage to be one man and one woman who leave their parents and build a new life together. Therefore, all the blessings associated with this institution are based on his instructions. Second, it's important because in Ephesians 5:31–32, Paul described marriage as a reflection of the relationship between Christ and his church. This has tremendous implications for the way we should approach marriage. I could not be more encouraged that you want your marriage to reflect the love Jesus has for his church. It is my prayer that this book will help you move toward Christlikeness and marital oneness.

I'm conscious that readers of this book will come from many different backgrounds. They may be at different places spiritually as they begin this book. What about you? Perhaps you were raised in the church since you were a baby and you've been pretty steady as a Christian all your life. Or perhaps you grew up in the church but you've had your struggles in your relationship with God. You may be someone who came to Christ after many years of living for other things, some of which you deeply regret. Or Christianity may be very new to you, and you largely have your fiancé(e) to thank for it. As you think about marriage, God can meet you where you are, no matter where that is, if you are willing to listen. If your heart is open to him and to his Word, he can take you from where you are to where you need to be, with him and with your future spouse. For that to happen, you may need to set aside some assumptions you've always had about marriage. Let me begin by encouraging you to avoid two extremes when thinking about married life.

Two Extremes

The first extreme is the belief that marriage has to be hard and difficult, with an inevitably miserable transition period. I firmly believe that God gave us the gift of marriage as one of the joys of life on earth. We don't need to enter it thinking that it will be anything other than wonderful. So please disregard those who act as if marriage is a tremendous burden, leading to struggle upon struggle. Yes, some marriages struggle, but God intends any struggles you have to show you where you need Jesus's work in your heart. He will show you how to rely on him for the love, strength, and wisdom you need to love your spouse well. God designed marriage as a blessing and, though we still struggle as sinners, we have access to God's grace in Jesus. That makes all the difference as we learn to live in the intimate relationship of marriage.

The second extreme to avoid is the belief that marriage will be wonderful without any effort. As one of my friends once told me, he thought the formula to a great marriage was really simple: Just "don't have sex before you are married, marry a Christian, and everything will be great." Certainly, the Bible encourages believers to only marry believers and to abstain from sex before marriage, but those things alone do not guarantee a wonderful marriage! They are not the sum total of the Christian life. We need to remember that Jesus taught us to be continuously dependent on him, because as sinners we need to be. He said, "Apart from me you can do nothing" (John 15:5). This misguided assumption, like the first one, results in many disappointments and frustrations if we hold onto it.

A more biblical approach is to recognize that God has given us marriage to enjoy. He created it for our pleasure, and he created it to give us a glimpse of his covenant love for us. But marriage also takes a commitment—a commitment to sacrifice for the benefit of someone else for the glory of God. It means living all of the ten thousand little moments of your life as if the glory of God and the preeminence of Jesus were at stake. If that sounds intimidating, it should! It is meant to take us where God always wants us to go—to Christ, in humble reliance on his power and promises to transform us into the people he redeemed us to be.

Goals for This Study

First, I want to help you establish a marriage that brings pleasure to Christ and to you. Therefore, this resource talks very little about the marriage ceremony. The ceremony is important, but I am far more interested in the lifetime of marriage that comes afterward. I often remind couples that I care a little about their wedding day, but I care a lot about the fifty (or more!) years that follow. So the focus of this book will be on how to build a life together with Jesus at the center.

Second, I believe that the best way to work through this material is with a pastor or a spiritually mature friend—a mentor. There is plenty that you can learn on your own, but many of us (myself included) are slow to identify areas where we struggle. We are even slower to do something about them without some form of personal encouragement and exhortation. It's much easier to pretend that those struggles don't exist—or at least aren't a big deal. But if you are willing to work with a mentor, it's much more likely that he will help you see your areas of blindness. Those realizations can be a bit painful or embarrassing at first, but they are for your good in the long run. So I hope that you'll allow this material to be more than something on your to-do list. Make it a first step in a journey of God-honoring change.

Third, this material is relevant whether you are twenty-one years old, about to be married for the first time, or whether you are fifty with three children, planning another wedding. It has something to offer if you've been widowed after a happy marriage or divorced after a tragic betrayal. It offers hope to a new believer with few good role models just as it does to someone from a stable Christian home. So let me encourage you to be teachable through this process. In each case there are lessons to be learned to make a new relationship work well. I want to help you learn whatever you need to learn for a lifetime of marriage.

Are you ready to begin? The eight chapters in this book describe eight areas that are crucial to establishing a marriage that honors Christ, resulting in great joy for both of you. Each chapter concludes with questions you will first answer yourself. Then you will compare and discuss your answers with your future spouse. Later, you will share them with the person who is mentoring you.

Before Your First Session

Before your first meeting with your mentor, you and your fiancé(e) should gather four things to help your mentor serve you effectively. I recommend doing this before you begin the first chapter.

1. Parental support

At our church we ask engaged couples, especially those being married for the first time, whether they have parental support for their marriage. There are a few reasons why we ask about this. First, we believe it is wise and helpful to have people who care about you, love you, and want the best for you to encourage your marriage. There is value in receiving input from those who care most about us.

A second reason is derived from Ephesians 6:2–3, which explains that everyone has the responsibility to honor their parents. In most cases, there will be parental contact after the wedding; gaining their support now helps to reinforce the relationships. Parental involvement and support lay a foundation for a family culture that communicates, cares, loves, and seeks to bless one another. You will see the benefits during the wedding planning and also in the years to come.

However, you may be in a situation where you cannot get parental support. Your parents may have died. Your parents may not be involved in your life, or you may have parents who reject Jesus and want their children to reject him as well. There are any number of possible scenarios here. If you are in such a situation, I offer two suggestions. First, please speak with your mentor, the person meeting with you and your fiancé(e) as you go through this book. Your mentor will help you think about your particular circumstances to determine the most godly approach. Second, consider asking someone you love and trust in your church family to serve in that role for you. Such individuals certainly do not carry the same level of authority as parents, but they can be a huge blessing to you, especially in an area of your life where there is hurt and pain. I have seen several young women develop relationships with a family in the church who served as unofficial "surrogate parents" as potential boyfriends came to call. For the young woman, this relationship provided protection from young men who lacked good intentions, and it also supported and encouraged her when a man of godly character came along. If you are older, friends, adult children, or small group leaders can serve in this role for you. The point is that all of us, regardless of age, are helped in our preparation for marriage (one of life's most important decisions) by having family and friends give their support.

2. Physical standards of conduct

Most, if not all, couples want to get married because they enjoy being together. They are physically attracted to each other, and being around the other person makes them happy. This is as it should be. In fact, we ought to seriously question why a couple would want to marry if sexual attraction was not present. But it is easy to move from enjoying one another to enjoying one another *too much*, especially since our culture tells us that premarital sex is essential to find out if you are compatible.

I have ministered to many newlywed couples and seen the damage that going too far physically has done to the relationship. It sets patterns of selfishness and pleasure-seeking (in the wrong ways at the wrong time) that are often hard to break. Those selfish issues rear their ugly heads in the form of significant conflict weeks, and sometimes days, after the ceremony.

For that reason, I ask all couples (even older ones) to write up their standards for the physical contact they will have during their engagement. Granted, the document does not remove temptation or control the heart. But standards are tools that can help couples live in a way that they will not be ashamed to discuss later. A friend once told me how difficult it had been for him to tell the woman he wanted to marry that he had been engaged before—and sexually active during that time. With tears he confessed that he wished he had waited for her. After all, sometimes engagements do not last.

3. Testimonies of conversion to Christ

The third thing you need is a written testimony of how you came to trust in Christ as your Savior and Lord. How did the Lord draw you to himself? Were you in a church for years when suddenly it "clicked"? Were you invited to a Vacation Bible School, a Bible study, or an Easter service? Did you have lots of questions and, slowly but surely, the Lord put someone in your life to answer them?

This exercise has many benefits. First, it helps you focus on the incomparable gift of eternal life that God offers us. We should never stop being awestruck that Jesus Christ, the sinless Son of God, would die on a cross for our benefit. Second, writing out your testimony sets the stage for our first lesson about putting Jesus at the center of your life and marriage. This concept will be emphasized again and again so that you become convinced that if you get the "Jesus part" right, everything else can work. But if Jesus is not the center of your life and your marriage, your foundation is gone and you are in danger. Third, as amazing as this seems, some couples preparing for marriage have never heard the conversion story of their future spouse. Reading each other's testimonies will encourage you; you may even learn something about your fiancé(e) that you did not know before!

4. Two paragraphs on why you want to marry your fiancé(e)

When I mentor engaged couples, I find it interesting to hear why they want to be married. What is it about her that encourages you to choose her for life? Of all the men in the universe (like three billion of them!), why him? Two paragraphs explaining your answer will clarify your thoughts and offer insights for your mentor.

I realize that these four tasks will be very simple for some, but very challenging for others. If you are a new Christian just learning about the Bible, or emerging from a difficult past, I want you to know that this book was written with you in mind just as much as it was written for someone who grew up in the church. The journey this book leads you through is not a journey about perfection. It is a journey about growth, one step at a time. Your mentor will help you each step of the way. Even if you take a few extra weeks to cover certain topics, please do not get discouraged. Even if there are times when you feel inadequate or like a failure, remember that it is our inadequacies and our failures that Jesus came to redeem. Take heart and have courage! I have never seen a couple work through this material and regret it. Each one found things of value and grew along the way. Yes, a few felt like quitting from time to time but, as they stuck with it, they valued the experience and the lessons they learned all the more.

Once you've gathered these four pieces of information (or at least done your best), it's time to begin the first lesson. Have a great time studying and learning together! The format of this study is very simple. Begin by reading the chapter. At the end of each chapter are a series of questions that you should first complete on your own. When each of you have finished, meet with your fiancé(e) to talk about your answers. Your mentor will also go over certain questions and concepts with you to guide and encourage you as you move toward marriage. May God bless you and keep you both!

Chapter 1
Jesus Must Be the Center of Your Life

And he said to him, "You shall love the Lord your God with
all your heart and with all your soul and with all your mind.
This is the great and first commandment. And a second is
like it: You shall love your neighbor as yourself. On these
two commandments depend all the Law and the Prophets."
(Matthew 22:37–40)

JESUS EXPLAINS THAT the greatest commandment is to love the
Lord your God with all your heart, soul, and mind. The three terms
of "heart," "soul," and "mind" are very similar in meaning. They
each refer to the command center of your life. Jesus uses the three
terms together for emphasis. The Lord wants you to love him with
everything you have. There can be no compartment of your life or
area of your heart that is off limits to him. One of the most important preparations for a Christ-centered marriage is to remember
that your affections belong first to Christ. You must love him with
all that you have and are.

The second commandment is similar: Love your neighbor as
yourself. This is not a call to love yourself—the Bible assumes that
you will do that just fine! The concern is whether you will transfer
this same concern to others. You know firsthand how easy it is to
love yourself and to develop friendships with people who like what

you like. But it's oh, so much harder to do so with people who are not like you. While you have likely concluded that you and your fiancé(e) have much in common, I can promise you that it is amazing how much you will learn about loving each other in the days ahead.

This passage from Matthew's Gospel identifies our top priorities. In one sense, Jesus says that if you really understand these two commands, you understand the entire Old Testament! (That is one amazing version of *CliffsNotes*!) In two simple yet profound commands, Jesus explains his priority system. Take the next few moments and let that sink in, especially the first command. *Your most important task in life is to love the Lord with everything you have.*

Engaged couples are often quick to talk about their love for each other. Surely, the two of you are reading this book because you have deep affection for each other. You have enjoyed many wonderful times together and are eagerly looking to take your relationship to the next level. In fact, during this time of your life, you often find yourself thinking about your future spouse, what you will do on your honeymoon, what your life will be like, and similar thoughts. However, one mistake that engaged couples make is to think that their relationship is the most important one of all. When they believe their most important relationship is their own, they make decisions based on that priority. You might even be tempted to attend a small group, Sunday school class, or Bible study simply to arrange for some premarital counseling. This is a dangerous line of thinking. If you treat your church, your pastors, or your friends as if *you* are the center of the universe, this will feed your selfishness, a selfishness that will be unleashed on your spouse (and others) in the days and weeks to come.

Please notice that Jesus says in Matthew 22 that the order of the commands is really important. Each of you was designed by God to love him *first*. When you function according to your purpose, you function at maximum capacity. But when Jesus is not at the center, you become like a pair of pliers trying to embed a nail in a piece of wood. You might be successful with enough time and determination, but a hammer would have been so much better! But when you love the Lord first, you function as you are designed to, and the results are amazing. You will not only experience a joyous relationship with the God of heaven and earth, but you will also be in a perfect position to enjoy all that God has designed marriage to be.

Motivations to Love the Lord with All Your Heart, Soul, and Mind

Motivation 1: Jesus died for you

It is possible to read the Bible without making much practical application to your life. However, that's not how God wants you to read his Word. Take, for example, Matthew 26–28, the story of Christ's crucifixion. You could read it much like you might read an account of the Holocaust. You might experience deep sadness as you read about the innocent dying. You might experience shock and disgust at the brutality leveled by a group of human beings on another. You might experience anger as you reflect on an individual's desire for absolute power. But it is possible to read about the Holocaust without it changing your life personally. And it is possible to do the same thing with the story of Jesus. The Lord, however, wants you to read the story differently.

He wants you to see his love for you. Peter betrays him three times and leaves to cry in shame. But Peter is the one Jesus comes to, restoring their relationship and calling him to serve him (see John 21). The kind of love Jesus had for Peter is also on display in Jesus's ministry to one of the thieves crucified with him. After the man confesses his faith in Jesus as Savior, Jesus promises, "Today you will be with me in Paradise" (Luke 23:43). That kind of love is offered to us too. Paul reminds us in Romans 5:8 that while we were sinners, Christ died for us. In other words, Jesus did not die for us because we were his loyal, faithful followers; he died while we were rebels, his enemies. The cross was bloody, gory, and shameful, a symbol of brutality and the worst of human experience. Yet the cross is beautiful because it was a place of grace, compassion, and salvation because of God's love for us.

The Lord's love for you is so deep that Jesus took upon himself the wrath of God that you deserved because of your sin. Matthew 27:46 is one of the most amazing passages in the Bible and one of my favorites. It says that Jesus cried out to God, "My God, my God, why have you forsaken me?" Jesus said that so that you would never have to—ever.

Motivation for living as a Christian does not come from trying to appease a God who wants to make life difficult for you. It comes when you remember the message of the cross, when you remember that Jesus died so that you might live. It comes when you remember that Jesus paid the debt he did not owe because you owed a debt you could not pay.

The death of Jesus should motivate you to thankfulness and love. In fact, it should motivate you to love him with all your heart, soul, and mind.

Motivation 2: Jesus gave you a new identity

The Scriptures teach that when a person trusts in Christ as Savior, he or she is given an entirely new identity. Words and phrases like "new" and "born again" are frequently used to describe the New Testament Christian. But the theme of identity is actually much more comprehensive. You might think of the gospel the way newly engaged women think about their diamond ring. It is fun to watch them suddenly use their left hand for all sorts of tasks that previously would have been done with their right hand or not done at all. Clearly, they want to show off their new "rock"! Not only do they show it off, they also carefully investigate the way the light affects it from multiple angles. They buy cleaning kits to keep their diamond in sparkling condition.

In many ways, the gospel is like that diamond. To appreciate its glory, you have to investigate it from all sides; each side contributes to the overall brilliance of the whole. From one direction, we see redemption—how in one moment God rescued us from sin by paying the penalty our sins deserved, which is death. Fans of Narnia see this when Aslan dies so that Edmund the traitor might go free. A slight change in perspective moves our focus to adoption. Yet another turn in our consideration of the gospel highlights our freedom in Christ—freedom from the tyranny of sin's penalty and power in our lives. With each successive "turn" of the gospel message, we see another aspect of its brilliance.

When these themes are brought together, the new identity Jesus gives is much more brilliant than any diamond. Here is a picture of that identity:

- You are redeemed from the slave market of sin (Galatians 3:13);
- You are adopted into God's family, no longer a spiritual orphan (Galatians 4:7);
- You are God's friend instead of his enemy (John 15:13–14);
- You are reconciled to God instead of separated from him (2 Corinthians 5:18);
- You are free instead of bound to the power and penalty of sin (Romans 6:12–19);
- You are prayed for instead of ignored (Romans 8:34);
- You are in God's presence, no longer alone (Hebrews 13:5);
- You are loved by God instead of alienated (Romans 8:35–39);
- You are regenerated, alive instead of dead (Ephesians 2:1–4);
- You are rescued from God's wrath over sin rather than receiving it (1 Thessalonians 1:10).

The identity Jesus gave us is not intended to make us proud, but to make us humble. It is not intended to make us think about ourselves, but to make us thankful for all that Jesus has done for us. It is not to draw attention to us, but to reflect praise and glory to Jesus. In fact, this new identity is what leads and calls us to love the Lord with all our heart, soul, and mind.

Motivation 3: Jesus provides all the spiritual resources you need to love, serve, and give

One passage that has become quite dear to me is Romans 8:31–35. It not only helps me in my marriage, it helps me in my life.

> What then shall we say to these things? If God is for us, who can be against us? He who did not spare his own Son but gave him up for us all, how will he not also with him graciously give us all things? Who shall bring any charge against God's elect? It is God who justifies. Who is to condemn? Christ Jesus is the one who died—more than that, who was raised—who is at the right hand of God, who indeed is interceding for us. Who shall separate us from the love of Christ? Shall tribulation, or distress, or persecution, or famine, or nakedness, or danger, or sword? (Romans 8:31–35)

A brief examination of this text can help explain the third motivation. I draw three statements out of this passage.

1. You need nothing. Verses 31–32 explain that if God was willing to give you his Son, he will be willing to give you all the spiritual resources you need as a believer. Did you notice the rhetorical question, "How will he not also with him graciously give us all things?" He will, of course he will! He already gave you his most prized possession. The "hard part" was giving his Son; the easy part is providing all other spiritual resources. What a promise! This brings healing to the hurting soul. If you have a rough background, this is an incredible promise. The Lord says that your prior sin or struggle does not stand in the way of his love or his promises. This should encourage you, give you hope, and empower you to live in a whole new way. You are not bound to your past or to the way in which you were raised.

This truth also helps us when we need to battle selfishness. For example, when I return home from a day at the office, I don't need my wife to give to me. I don't need my children to serve me. In fact, I don't need anything! Jesus has already provided everything I need. My "love tank," so to speak, is full of the love that comes from the Lord. It is a love that satisfies, protects, secures, and comforts. This allows me as a Christian husband to love with the love given to me by the Lord.

Think about what happens if your love tank is not full from the Lord. What happens if you really don't believe that the Lord is providing all the necessary resources? I suggest that you would demand love from your spouse. It may start out subtly, or war may immediately break out with nuclear weapons. Either way, you will discover that you expect your spouse to make you happy. You expect your spouse to give you what you want in the marriage. In my own life and in counseling, I have noticed that the love we demand from others is not satisfying. It demands more and more and more.

What I love so much about these verses is that they teach me that I have everything I need already. This is freeing. No more demanding. No more manipulating. No more clamoring after what I need. After all, I need nothing that Jesus has not already given me. And neither do you.

2. Jesus's opinion is the one that matters. Verses 33–34 are just as profound as verses 31–32. This section focuses on the one who can justify and the one who can condemn. Let's face it—some questions are more important than others! In this case, Jesus is answering the ones that are most important. Your boss's opinion may count a lot when it comes to the quality of your work. Your spouse's opinions about the way you treat her are important to your relationship. But when it comes to matters of justification and condemnation, Jesus gets to talk and everyone else gets to be quiet. This is particularly important because there will always be people who put you down. There will always be people who make you feel worthless. But in the end, they all get to be quiet and the one who condemns and justifies gets to speak. What Jesus says matters! Thankfully, he is the one who died for us and the one who has given us our new identity.

It would be nice if your spouse never said a mean thing to you as long as you live. But you know that there will be (or have been) moments when you struggle as a couple. So expect some grief, disappointment, and frustration in your marriage. When those moments come, remind yourself that Jesus's word is most important. And he can use those struggles to help you both trust him more and become more like him.

This point is also true as you think about your past experiences. There may be people in your life who knew you when you were living a wild and crazy life. They may ridicule your faith or tell you that you are nothing. But once again Jesus's promises bring healing to the hurting soul. You are not bound by their words or their opinions. Jesus's opinion is the one that really matters.

3. You are secure. Verse 35 emphasizes the reality of security. Notice that in the text there is not a "who" or a "what" that can ever separate you from the love of God in Christ. This is such a wonderful assurance! It tells you that you have security. Personally, I long for security at work, in my marriage, and in all my relationships. But sometimes those human relationships do not seem very secure. In a heated argument, one person can say something that threatens security ("I wish I had not married you!"). In other cases, a spouse does something that threatens security (e.g., gets caught looking at pornography). But in your relationship with Jesus there is complete security. The Old Testament often speaks of God being our rock, our fortress, our salvation, and our strong deliverer. Romans 8 makes it clear that Jesus is our rock and our stability even when other relationships seem anything but stable.

This passage reminds you that the Lord has poured out his love for you. Jesus died for you. Jesus has given you a new identity. Jesus has provided ongoing resources for every day of your life. So rather than demand love from your spouse, you are free to give it. You will find that when you recognize the Lord's satisfying, comforting, and protecting love, you will find joy and peace. Ironically, you will also discover more joy, encouragement, and happiness in your marriage. To top it off, you will learn to love the Lord with all your heart, mind, and strength.

Motivation 4: Jesus is your spouse's only hero

I want to be important to my wife. I want her to see me as a knight in shining armor (even if I don't live up to it). I want her to think of me as her man, but I am also painfully aware that no matter how nice I have been to her, no matter how caring, no matter how loving, I can never save her soul. Thus my love and care, while meaningful, is not the ultimate love and care my wife receives. Over time I have grown to love this truth. I do not have to be Stephanie's savior; I am free to be her husband. This takes so much pressure off me! In fact, in those moments when something happens that I (or anyone for that matter) cannot fix, she can run to her hero Jesus—and I can go too. Jesus makes her happy. He comforts her. He encourages her soul. These same comments work for Stephanie as well. When I encounter a challenging issue in life, she does not have to fix it. She can love me and point me to Jesus.

The fact that Jesus is your spouse's only hero is yet one more reason to love the Lord your God with all your heart, soul, and mind. You see, your love for your fiancé(e) will be directly related to your love for Jesus. When Jesus is at the center of your life, he will be your rock, your fortress, and your strong deliverer. This will mean, among other things, that your future spouse will not have to serve in that role. I can be, and must be, a Christian husband to my wife, but I can never be her savior or her hero. That is a title reserved for Jesus alone.

Loving the Lord First Is Central to a Marriage That Accurately Represents Christ and the Church

Reason 1: Marital happiness or marital struggle often can be summarized in the word "worship."

The counseling center at Faith Church in Lafayette, Indiana (where I serve as a pastor) has existed since 1978. In those years of counseling, there have been lots of marriage cases. All of those couples started out much like you and your fiancé(e). There were two people who believed they loved each other, enjoyed spending time together, and fostered dreams together. But at some point, things changed for our counselees. They were no longer living in marital bliss. Instead, there was heartache, pain, and deep struggle. As we met with them, some would blame the state of their marriage on poor communication, some would talk about problem-solving challenges, others would talk about pornography, an emotional affair, a physical affair, or a challenge with a child. The couples were convinced that these issues were the real problem. If only they had a few tools or tips, things would be much better!

While our counselees were correct that there were problems with communication, pornography, or problem solving, there are also much deeper concerns. Jesus taught that what comes out in our words and actions is always based on what is already on the inside, in our hearts.

"For out of the heart come evil thoughts, murder,
adultery, sexual immorality, theft, false witness, slander."
(Matthew 15:19)

Behind the struggles with poor communication, problem solving, or understanding the roles of husband and wife, there were struggles because of poor worship. Remember that we were designed to worship God and love him most. If he is not the focus of our worship, then something else will be. Idolatry did not work out so well for the nation of Israel and it will not work out well for us either. You will find that worship is the underlying heart issue, while poor communication, problem solving, porn, or children are natural by-products of a heart worshiping something other than the Lord Jesus.

You were designed to worship the Lord. When you, as a couple or as an individual, worship something other than the Lord, the field of discord is prepared. Jesus must be the center of your life and the center of your relationship.

Reason 2: When you love Jesus, you will be most prepared to love your spouse.

In John 15:11, Jesus reminds his disciples that his love for them would result in their joy being complete. In verse 18 he explains that his love will help the disciples love others even when they are hated. In John 15, Jesus has been explaining the importance of abiding or remaining in him. He was helping his disciples understand that, to carry out their purpose, they had to receive the nourishment found in the vine. When the Christian is nourished by the love of Christ, he or she is capable of loving others, even when the context is unpleasant.

Engaged couples do not tend to think this way. You, like many others, may have experienced a relatively problem-free engagement.

The thought of looking at one another with disdain is foreign to you. However, if you are removed from the life-giving nourishment of Christ the Vine, it will not be long before criticism and conflict follow. Loving others, including your spouse, will be much easier when you love the Lord first.

Reason 3: To be a Christian spouse, you must first be a faithful Christian.

This sounds logical, but many miss the significance of this point. I sometimes hear men and women speak about their boyfriends or girlfriends as "he/she is Christian" as if there were no other questions to ask. But there is a big difference between a person who *says* he is a Christian and a person with a proven track record of putting Christ first in his life. There is an interesting progression in Ephesians 4–6. In chapter 4 there is an emphasis on each Christian growing as a faithful person. In chapter 5 there is an emphasis on learning to be a faithful partner, and at the beginning of chapter 6 there is a focus on being a faithful parent. I believe that this progression is intentional. Some try to mix up the order and it simply does not work. One says he wants to be a faithful Christian husband, but he has not yet learned what it means to be a faithful Christian—to be committed to Christ and dependent on him for the strength to walk in his ways. As we will see in future chapters, husbands and wives have responsibilities to each other that they do not have to anyone else. Those responsibilities are much more intense and require much more sacrifice. It will be easy to offer excuses as to why you should not fulfill them. But when someone talks this way, he or she is expressing a fundamental problem with his or her heart. Before a person can be a faithful Christian partner, he or she must first be a faithful Christian individual. The Bible is clear: Love God first, then love your neighbor as yourself. Your closest neighbor is your spouse.

Putting Christ at the center of your life is not primarily a focus on your marriage. It is first a commitment to live as a biblical Christian.

Conclusion

Jesus must be the center of your life. You are called to love Jesus with all your heart, soul, and mind. He must have first place in your heart, even above your fiancé(e), if your marriage is to glorify God and exemplify Christ's relationship with the church. As you prepare for a strong and lasting marriage, the first step is to ensure that your walk with Christ is strong enough to enjoy the blessings of covenant marriage and endure its challenges. Step one is about being a Christian. Only then can you be a Christian husband or Christian wife.

Homework Discussion Questions

Complete the following questions on your own and then share your answers with your fiancé(e). Later, discuss your answers and your conversation as a couple with your mentor.

Your mentor will help you understand the purpose of each question, but let me explain one assignment that I ask you to do in every chapter: place a passage of Scripture on an index card and review it daily. Many believers, both new and old, struggle to know passages of the Bible. They know *about* the Bible, but they do not know many passages directly. The goal of this assignment is for each of you to have a set of eight to ten index cards with crucial passages that can serve you well your entire life. This assignment is not busy work. It is an assignment that has changed my life and the lives of many couples I have counseled.

Let me encourage you to think deeply about these questions. Shallow answers will hurt you and your future spouse more than anyone else. Deeper, more honest answers may lead to some uncomfortable moments, but that is okay. These real-life discussions will help you prepare and learn as a couple.

1. Are there areas of your life that you have not yet given over to the Lord, the one who loves you more than anyone? If so, identify them and explain why they have been hard to relinquish.

2. On a scale of 1–10, how would you rate your personal, daily walk with Jesus? What evidence could you give to justify your rating (e.g., "I regularly read the Word," "I serve weekly in children's ministry," "I have no secret sins," and "I actively pursue relationships in the church that encourage me to have Jesus as the center of my life")?

3. On a scale of 1–10, how would you rate your fiancé(e)'s personal, daily walk with Jesus? What evidence justifies your rating? (If the way you rate your future spouse is substantially different from the way he or she rates him- or herself—and vice versa—please discuss it as a couple and then with your mentor.)

4. As you read this chapter, what three statements had the most impact on you? Be prepared to discuss this as a couple and with your mentor.

5. Skim this chapter again and choose the Bible passage that is most significant to you. Put it on an index card and review it daily until your appointment with your mentor.

6. Give at least one example from the last week or so when you were frustrated in your relationship with your fiancé(e). How did thinking about the gospel and what Jesus did for you help you to respond with grace, love, and compassion? If it didn't help, why do you think it didn't?

7. As a response to this chapter's call to make Jesus the center of your life, list two action steps you need to begin right away. Possibilities include personal devotions, dedicated prayer time, service in your local church, more faithful giving, etc.

8. Spend at least five minutes daily praying for yourself and your fiancé(e), that Jesus would truly be the center of your lives.

Advanced Homework

Here are two homework possibilities that you as a couple may find encouraging and beneficial.

1. Read John 15:1–16 each day for five days in a row. Make at least three thoughtful comments about the importance of putting Jesus in the center of your life.

2. Read *A Gospel Primer for Christians* by Milton Vincent (Bemidji, MN: Focus Publishing, 2008). There is a short devotional version that may be helpful. If you have the full-length book, write three observations about the importance of the gospel in your everyday life on a notecard to carry with you and review at least twice a day for a week. This will help you keep a Christ-centered perspective on your life.

Chapter 2

Love with Jesus as the Center

> If I speak in the tongues of men and of angels, but have not love, I am a noisy gong or a clanging cymbal. And if I have prophetic powers, and understand all mysteries and all knowledge, and if I have all faith, so as to remove mountains, but have not love, I am nothing. If I give away all I have, and if I deliver up my body to be burned, but have not love, I gain nothing.
>
> Love is patient and kind; love does not envy or boast; it is not arrogant or rude. It does not insist on its own way; it is not irritable or resentful; it does not rejoice at wrongdoing, but rejoices with the truth. Love bears all things, believes all things, hopes all things, endures all things. (1 Corinthians 13:1–7)

YOU KNOW THAT love is important for any relationship, especially marriage. The apostle Paul wrote these words about love in the midst of a longer conversation about spiritual gifts. Paul was concerned that some folks in the Corinthian church were considered better than others simply because they were able to serve in certain ways. In that context, the Lord, through Paul, gave instruction not only to a church that existed 2,000 years ago, but also to us. Whenever we serve, we must do so from a heart of love. Any service without it is like a noisy gong; it is nothing, and has no eternal value. This concept is powerful not only in the church but in marriage, which God designed to reflect Christ's relationship to his church.

I am fairly confident that you and your fiancé(e) are convinced that you love each other. You wouldn't be pursuing marriage if you didn't. Nevertheless, it is still profitable to consider the biblical descriptions and characteristics of love. You may learn more than you expected!

Love According to the World

Let's begin by considering how our society talks about the concept of love when applied to a romantic relationship. (I use this qualification because these same elements are not applied to other loving relationships. For example, love as physical attraction is not the way the world would describe a mother's love for her children. In that case, common grace still rules and love is described in terms of self-sacrifice, service, and giving.)

Love is a warm, fuzzy feeling

Our society encourages us to believe that love is primarily a feeling—a warm, tingly feeling. Some may describe it as a rise in temperature when she enters the room. Some speak about how their heart rate changes or how they begin to sweat. This sounds good until those feelings begin to disappear. The couple begins to speak about the past as the time they were "in love"; now they feel like they are just roommates. The "love" is gone and there is nothing left of their relationship. Some, in the absence of these feelings, decide that they need to find their true soulmate elsewhere. The concern here is the number of unhappy, unwanted, and broken marriages that exist because love, at least in the couples' minds, is simply a feeling.

Love is physical attraction

Another definition equates love with physical "chemistry" or sexual attraction, that sense of pleasure and anticipation at the thought of being intimate with another person. Surely, God designed human beings to enjoy pleasure, including sexual pleasure within marriage. But this was not all that marriage was intended to be.

One of the most obvious biblical examples of the flaws in this perspective is Samson. Samson pursued several women because he was sexually attracted to them and it ultimately resulted in chaos. This was true with his first wife (Judges 13) and with Delilah. But Samson is not the only illustration. Scripture gives lots of examples of sexual attraction that has nothing to do with love and everything to do with selfishness and lust. David and his sin with Bathsheba is another classic illustration. The Bible tells us that David saw her bathing and was attracted to her (2 Samuel 11). In each case, when love was merely defined as physical attraction, hurt, pain, and suffering were the ultimate result. Our society offers plenty of sad confirmations of that reality. Thus, while we certainly expect and hope that you are physically attracted to your fiancé(e), attraction alone is not an adequate definition of love.

Love is having fun together

Others describe love as having fun together. Again, it would be strange if two people wanted to marry because they hated each other and enjoyed fighting! But when love is reduced to having fun together, what happens when life isn't fun? I grew up with a sister who could not walk on her own. She had birth defects that left her with no feeling in her legs. She was not mentally disabled, but she was a special needs child. As my parents cared for her, they discovered that many parents of special needs children divorced. A spouse believed that life was too hard and sought greener pastures elsewhere. They were not having fun and their definition of love was inadequate for the life they were leading. The love they thought they had did not endure when the fun of doing whatever one wanted was replaced with the hard work of parenting a special needs child.

Have you been influenced by any of these definitions? It's pretty hard not to be, in this society. And against that backdrop, the feelings you have for each other may have convinced you that you truly love each other. But think about it: If your definition of love is little more than the warm fuzzies, physical attraction, and the ability to have fun together, your relationship may demonstrate *not* how much you love the other person, but how much you each love *yourself*! What you have found is a person who helps you love *you* better than anyone else has! That is a sobering and scary thought.

But it is also a very helpful thought. The Lord may be showing you that your definition is lacking so that your heart can see your need to depend on Christ for the love you need to give your spouse. He may be softening you in order to show you "the more excellent way" of true biblical love (1 Corinthians 12:31). And by his Holy Spirit, he can empower you to love your fiancé(e) with that true biblical love. This chapter will give you ample opportunity to evaluate your love for your future spouse, to talk about it with your mentor, and to encourage your growth in biblical love by relying on Christ's power and the change he made in you when you first trusted in him.

Love According to the Bible

First Corinthians 13 gives us a profound and practical picture of biblical love. The characteristics of love given there do not represent the sum total of biblical love, but this chapter is one of the most extended discussions of love found anywhere in the Bible.

Love is patient

We learned in our last chapter that all believers in Christ have been given a new identity when they put their faith in Jesus. God sees us through the finished work of Christ. We also saw that God promised us many blessings in Christ that impact our lives each day ("I need nothing, Jesus's word is the one that matters, and I am secure"). However, I think we would all admit that we still sin and we are sinned against. When we sin, we are still tempted to minimize it or pretend that it does not exist. When we are sinned against, we are tempted to make a big deal about it. That is why marriages all across our world are in disarray. Each person minimizes his own sin and maximizes the sin of others.

Love that is motivated and empowered by Jesus responds differently. Biblical love responds with patience when it is tempted to be angry. Proverbs 19:11 captures this idea wonderfully: "Good sense makes one slow to anger, and it is his glory to overlook an offense." There have probably been times in your relationship already when you have been tempted to respond with sinful anger—and there will be many more times in your marriage. You will be tempted to justify your actions and carry them out quickly, convinced that you are right. Biblical love does not pursue such ends. It pursues patience even in the midst of difficulty or anger.

Even if one of you chooses to respond with anger, our identity in Christ still allows the other to respond with biblical love characterized by patience.

Love is kind

Patience is especially needed when one is hurt. It demonstrates a willingness to entrust the hurt to the Lord, to rely on his resources, and not lash out to protect itself. In that sense, its actions are passive in nature. Kindness, however, is an active idea. Oh, that marriage would be characterized by kindness! I know a man who told his wife on their honeymoon that he would be more attracted to her if she lost twenty pounds. Can you believe that? Can you imagine the hurt? No doubt she could forgive him, but that was a comment she will remember as long as the Lord gives her mental recall.

Biblical love is not characterized by a mere "I will do something nice for you if you do something nice for me." Biblical love demonstrates kindness. It looks for ways to be encouraging, complimentary, and affectionate even if the kindness is not immediately reciprocated. Young couples often focus on the fun things they do together, but their marriages would be much stronger if they chose to be more kind to each other, not just in the normal, mundane parts of life, but in the face of pain or hurt.

The good news is that we do not have to rely on our own resources to be kind or to respond in kindness when hurt. The grace of God can help us to be kind. The Lord told us to go confidently before the throne of grace to receive mercy and find grace to help in our time of need (Hebrews 4:16). I think the Lord tells us to go confidently because he wants us to come, so that he can say "Yes."

Love is not jealous

A third characteristic of biblical love is particularly powerful in its Corinthian context. Rivalry, competition, and factions developed, with each group seeking to win additional followers. One cannot miss the Lord's overwhelming condemnation of the church's willingness to be so divisive. That is particularly powerful in light of this characteristic of love.

Love that is not jealous is love that does not require first place. It allows another to succeed without reprisal. A humorous example of this is found in the DreamWorks Animation movie *Monsters vs. Aliens*. The movie opens as Derek, a local TV weatherman, and Susan are about to be married. Just before the ceremony, Susan has the misfortune of being hit by a meteor (!). A powerful substance enters her body, making her grow in size and strength to astronomical proportions. The wedding is interrupted and Susan makes it her mission to reunite with Derek. In the process, however, she learns that Derek was only interested in her as long as he was the one in the spotlight.

As we move to real life, the sad reality is that Derek's attitude is often not discovered until after the ceremony. One's desire to be the center of attention has not fully come to light, but it is there. In our world the focus is on who makes more money, whose job is more prestigious, and who is more gifted. In these moments and circumstances, jealousy is kindled. One spouse decides that he is sick of being in the shadow, playing second fiddle. Soon he finds ways to compete against his spouse and demonstrates that his love is jealous.

Love that is not jealous will celebrate the successes of the other person. It will compliment and support the gifts, skills, and abilities of the other person. Love that is not jealous will find ways to encourage the development of the other.

Love does not brag and is not arrogant

Let's take the same situation and add some names. Let's say that Julie and Tom were recently married. Tom is bright, handsome, and a mover and shaker at work. Julie works and does a good job, but she is neither as bright nor as gregarious as her husband. Julie must guard against jealousy. She must turn her heart to the Lord so that she does not get angry every time another woman glances in Tom's direction or every time he receives another commendation.

At the same time, Tom cannot be reminding Julie just how lucky she is to have him, since he had lots of other prospects. He cannot strive for the attention of other people, especially other women. He cannot compare his salary to hers and act like he is doing all the work. He cannot ask to be rewarded when he does something nice for Julie. He cannot explain to other couples that he is the prime example of love. This message was particularly powerful in a Corinthian church that was full of pride. The term "arrogant" was used five times to describe the Corinthian church itself. In a marriage, love does not go around explaining how wonderful it is.

Consider the example of Christ. He chose the path of humility before people who wrongly accused him. He chose the path of silence before the Roman governor. These responses seem impossible for us, and they are if we are only trusting in ourselves. Yet Ephesians 3:20–21 reminds us that Christ does far more than we can ever imagine through his great power that works in us. A person relying on Christ does not have to love with pride or arrogance.

Love does not act unbecomingly (is not rude)

I wish I had a dollar for every time one of my counselees was rude to the other. I am convinced that I could work for the church for free. Sometimes it comes in words, when one spouse says something that is not very nice to the other. Other times it comes in actions, when one spouse creates work for the other spouse. One person is simply being rude. Biblical love has no place for that. Biblical love chooses to be kind even when rude is tempting.

Love does not seek its own

While many people marry because the other person helps them love *themselves* better than anyone else, biblical love is interested in giving instead of taking, and serving instead of being served. When people arrive home from work, they often feel tired and run down. They are ready for a relaxing, problem-free evening. But when they are met at the door by a needy spouse (one who wants to have adult conversation for the next two hours, one who wants to share her feelings and emotions, one who is crying after a horrible day), there is a tendency to get frustrated. Biblical love does not demand from the other person, but willingly gives. Biblical love seeks the good of the other.

You might ask, "How does this happen?" Most of us, myself included, have a drive from our work to our home. A wise man uses this drive time to pray and confess something like this: "Lord, you know I am tired. What I want most is to go home and discover that the homework is done, a wonderful dinner is ready, and a relaxing evening of playing outside in the beautiful weather is ahead. But I know that your will might be something different today. Help me to remember that I don't need anything because you have given me everything I have to have. If I get home and chaos exists, help me to gently, kindly, patiently love each member of my family. Help me remember that my wife has probably had a hard day too and you may be calling me to serve her tonight. Please help me to use this opportunity to display the reality that Jesus's death, burial, resurrection, ascension, and present ministry are meaningful in my life."

Love is not easily provoked

Have you ever met someone who is "touchy"? I don't mean a person who likes to be physically connected. I am talking about a person who overreacts, so that you feel like you have to walk on eggshells around him. In our ministry we see couples like this regularly. They see the other person through lenses that filter out anything of value, leaving only those things that are harmful or annoying. They see the other person as the reason for their misery. This leads to provocation over the smallest matters. Biblical love matures far beyond such measures. To say that love is not easily provoked means that a person is willing to give grace even when tempted to respond with venom. It means that a person is willing to look at his or her spouse with lenses that see the good. For example, one married couple sought counseling over an argument. It turned out that the wife had wrongly prejudged her husband's motives and began attacking him. Once attacked, he became angry in return. Both were so used to seeing the wrong in the other person, they failed to consider the possibility that their assumptions were incorrect. Biblical love chooses patience over provocation.

Love does not keep a record of wrongs

My former pastor recounted a story where a couple, married about ten years, requested counseling. Jim and Karen, as we will call them, sat down at the first meeting and Karen presented a notebook outlining the ways Jim had failed, frustrated, irritated, or sinned against her during their marriage. There were pages upon pages. My pastor did not know their whole story, but in five minutes realized that Karen, at least, was a master record-keeper for failure (Jim's, anyway) and a pathetic historian of the positive elements. Jim and Karen were married, but they did not share biblical love, because biblical love does not keep records of wrongs. Karen kept an actual notebook where the wrongs were recorded, but many other couples use their minds instead. They don't write everything down, but they work to remember the wrongs that frustrate them and justify their own unloving responses.

Psalm 103:12 says of the Lord, "As far as the east is from the west, so far does he remove our transgressions from us." I am so thankful for that truth! It tells me that God wipes the slate clean and he keeps it clean. If the Lord kept track of my wrongs, it would fill more than a notebook and it would be hard to imagine how I could have a meaningful relationship with him. Just as the Lord keeps the slate clean, so can he help you do the same.

Love does not rejoice in unrighteousness but rejoices in the truth

Virtually all human relationships have elements that are positive and elements that are negative. People tend to focus on one or the other. The quality of the relationship is often determined by this outlook. For example, my wife may say that our marriage is perfect, but she is responding with biblical love and only focusing on the things that are right and consistent with biblical truth. It would not be true to say that everything about our relationship or my treatment of her is consistent with biblical truth, but her gracious evaluation excludes those elements. To use an analogy from education, my lowest scores are dropped and forgotten.

Love does not seek to discuss all the things that are wrong, but focuses on the things that are right. When God sees us through the righteousness of Christ, that is exactly what he does as well. He chooses to see what is good.

These characteristics of love are then summarized into four more general comments.

Love bears all things

God is saying that there is nothing love cannot handle. I wish more newlywed couples would refer to home as the location of their spouse rather than the location of their house. Biblical love can endure whatever God may allow into our lives. It can even make a relationship stronger in the midst of trouble. An engaged man in our church believed that his fiancée loved him. She proved it when she learned that his grandmother had been murdered. In that situation, she did not focus on her desires and wants. Instead, she simply chose to love her fiancé. She understood that his mind would be on his mom, his grandfather, his aunts and uncles, so she did not fight for attention. Instead, she chose to love him by encouraging him, being with him, and visiting with family members she had never met. She understood that she needed to comfort her fiancé. Her willingness to bear all things confirmed to him that his choice to marry her was a good one.

Love believes all things

Our ministry often cares for people who don't like being married anymore. One thing they find hard to do is to believe the best of their spouse. Biblical love is open and accepting. This does not mean that love is gullible or foolishly blind. However, spouses exercising biblical love are willing to risk being hurt again because of the love they have received from Christ. I often hear about the protective walls that people erect against the hurts that other people can cause. Inevitably these personal fortresses do not work and the relationship is all the worse for them. It is true that when there is a lot of hurt and pain in a relationship, it takes time for trust to be rebuilt. But one of the first steps on the pathway to trust is choosing to exhibit the quality of believing the best. Jesus is our rock and our fortress; that enables us to believe the best, even when we are tempted to think the worst.

Love hopes all things

At this stage of your relationship, you are likely filled with excitement about the present and the future. Your relationship is filled with hope. Fantastic! Your upcoming marriage should be filled with hope. However, most marriages experience some difficult times too. Sometimes sin is discovered in a person's life. In these cases, hope is crucial. To say that biblical love hopes all things implies that you will be willing to give your spouse another chance. That is exactly what God has done with us. Even the prophet Jonah was given multiple chances. This is made easier when you remember that you are a sinner as well, and when you believe in the power of God to change each of you. Thus, hope believes that all things, by the grace of God, are really possible in the relationship.

Love endures all things

It is possible, maybe even probable, that at some point during your married life you will struggle with hope. It may not be due to sin in the marriage; it may be due to an irreversible illness or a financial disaster. The previous point about love hoping all things will not be easy. In those moments, this last characteristic of love becomes so important. Love endures. You are able to love through it all. One of my mentors is Dr. Bob Smith. He helped to begin the counseling ministry at Faith in 1977. He served actively until 2012 when his wife's health required a change in priorities. They have been through many blessings and challenges in their sixty years of marriage. Some of those days were very hard, yet what we see is a testimony of joyful endurance.

The list in 1 Corinthians 13 seems overwhelming. Admittedly, it is a challenging list for anyone to do. However, while 1 Corinthians 13 says a lot about love, the Bible includes several other important additions. These additions, like the characteristics of 1 Corinthians 13, show how the Lord Jesus chose to love us. And as we rely on him, he can give us what we need to follow his example.

Jesus Loves by Giving

> "For God so loved the world, that he gave his only Son, that whoever believes in him should not perish but have eternal life." (John 3:16)

A couple of weeks ago you prepared for premarital counseling by writing why you want to be married. No doubt you recorded various traits and qualities that you appreciate in your fiancé(e), and I'm certainly glad you can articulate why you want to spend your life with this person. However, ultimately, that is not the best answer. You should want to get married because there is no one on planet Earth that you would rather give to than your fiancé(e). You cannot imagine sacrificing for anyone more than him or her. You cannot imagine giving more of yourself to anyone else. Strong and lasting marriages occur when both persons draw on the love that Jesus has poured out on them and share it with others.

Loving this way is not just a matter of your willpower. It comes from an awareness of your inability and a constant reliance on Christ, his Word, his promises, and his resources. We will not reach perfection this side of heaven, but we can continually take steps of growth.

Jesus Loves by Serving

"For even the Son of Man came not to be served but to serve, and to give his life as a ransom for many." (Mark 10:45)

Marriage is a picture of Jesus and the church. In Mark 10:45, Jesus explains his mission of service. The reason his armies do not fight is because Jesus's mission is not military rule. Jesus came to die, to give his life for many. In marriage, you are going to serve your spouse more than any other human being. You will often do things for the other simply because you want to serve him or her. Over time, you may serve your spouse in ways you never even imagined. This service does not have to be viewed as a burden. It can be seen as an opportunity to follow the example of our Lord. Since he has already done it, he is the perfect person to help us do the same.

Jesus Loves by Self-Sacrifice

"Greater love has no one than this, that someone lay down his life for his friends. You are my friends if you do what I command you. No longer do I call you servants, for the servant does not know what his master is doing; but I have called you friends, for all that I have heard from my Father I have made known to you." (John 15:13–15)

Dating is easy compared to marriage. In dating you can always go home, skip a day, and prepare to put your best foot forward next time. No such opportunity in marriage! Marriage puts people together at their best and at their worst. You are called to love in a sacrificial way. Jesus explains in John 15 that he is going to die for his friends. Deciding to be married is deciding to give yourself for another.

At this point, I hope you are a bit overwhelmed at the description of biblical love. I hope you see that there is no way you can possibly do this on your own. My wife and I married in September 1993. We are well past the twenty-year mark. Our marriage has never been characterized by fighting, intense arguing, vehement disagreements, or the like. It has, by God's grace, been a wonderful partnership functioning together as a team. But I would be a total liar if I said I loved my wife like this in all the little moments of our lives. There have been times when I have been demanding instead of giving, wanting to be served instead of serving, and wanting what I want with no regard for self-sacrifice. It will be that way for you as well. We are all still sinners. While we hope and trust that through the years we will grow more like Jesus, perfection only occurs in heaven. In the meantime, there is no way that you will love your future spouse like this without the ongoing grace and power that comes from the Lord Jesus.

It is so easy to read the first chapter of this book and agree with everything in it. It is so easy to proclaim on Sunday morning that Jesus is the center of your life. But when your spouse does or says something annoying, that moment—that moment right there—will be the moment that reveals your heart. Will the truth of Scripture reign? Will Jesus influence you in that moment? Or will biblical love be tossed out for one of the fake versions?

As a wife, what happens when your husband does not like the food you worked so hard to prepare? Your heart will show in that moment. You will either worship Jesus and love, or you will respond with anger and frustration because you wanted your husband to like what you prepared.

As a husband, what happens when your wife does not respect your opinion because her dad thinks differently? You will either worship Jesus and love her in that moment, or you will deliver your wrath to her. I could add illustration after illustration. Love is not what you profess at the matrimonial altar; it is what you do in the ten thousand little moments of your life.

Let me encourage you to go back to chapter 1. Read again the headings about your identity in Christ. Read again about the reasons why Jesus must be at the center. Commit to spend your life seeking to develop a meaningful relationship with Jesus and to live dependent on his grace. Ask the Lord to help you love as he loved.

Homework Discussion Questions

Complete the following questions on your own and then share your answers with your fiancé(e). Later, discuss your answers and your conversation as a couple with your mentor.

Think deeply about these questions. Shallow answers will hurt you and your future spouse more than anyone else. Deeper, more honest answers may lead to some uncomfortable moments, but that is okay. These real-life discussions will help you prepare and learn as a couple.

1. How has your definition of love been impacted by reading this chapter?
2. On a scale of 1–10, how would you rate your love, according to the biblical definition, for your future spouse? How would you prove your answer?
3. On a scale of 1–10, how would you rate your fiancé(e)'s love for you? What evidence justifies your rating? If your answers were substantially different from your fiancé(e)'s, discuss it and be ready to share with your mentor.

4. What three statements in this chapter had the most impact on you? What struck you about them? Be prepared to discuss with each other and with your mentor.

5. Skim this chapter and look for the Bible passage most significant to you. Put it on an index card and review it each day until your appointment with your mentor. (You should have two index cards at this point.)

6. Give at least two examples from the last month where, in your heart, you realized you wanted your own pleasure and encouraged your fiancé(e) to give it to you. How could those situations be changed to exhibit biblical love?

7. In response to this chapter, list two action steps that you need to begin right away to exhibit biblical love in your relationship with your fiancé(e).

8. Spend at least five minutes daily praying for yourself and your fiancé(e), that Jesus would truly be the center of your life and that your love for each other would be biblical.

Advanced Homework

Here is an additional homework possibility that you as a couple may find encouraging and beneficial.

• Read Matthew 26–28, the story of the death, burial, and resurrection of Jesus. Make at least three thoughtful comments about the character of Jesus's love for his people.

Chapter 3

Problem Solving
with Jesus as the Center

THE PURPOSE OF this book is to help you prepare for a lifelong, strong, and lasting marriage. Chapter 1 laid the foundation that Jesus must be the center of your life because that is our calling and our privilege as believers. And living as a Christian is essential to building a Christian marriage and family.

But we can only live this way by relying on the strength and grace God provides. The gospel hope that saved us is also what we rely on as we live out our new identity. We look to Jesus, our Creator and Redeemer, for all that we need to follow him. We talked about the fact that you and your fiancé(e) must love Jesus more than you love each other.

In chapter 2, we considered the fact that the Bible's description of love is something far beyond our ability as sin-prone, broken human beings. We must depend on Jesus daily if we ever hope to love in the way 1 Corinthians 13 describes. This means acknowledging our self-centeredness and repenting of it to the Lord, and asking for his love to transform us so that we can love others with that same love.

Now we turn our attention to another critical matter—problem solving. Have you ever seen any of the cable TV shows on hoarders?

Hoarders refuse to throw away anything. They not only save valuable and helpful things, they often save trash—and even take trash from others to satisfy their desire to acquire more things. In extreme cases, it is impossible to walk through the home without stepping on piles of filth. People healthy enough to be reading this book are unlikely to be featured on these TV shows, but you may be more like these hoarders than you realize.

Many of the couples I see in marriage counseling began just like you. They were excited about the possibilities of marriage and happy with each other. They could not imagine having any marital difficulties, let alone difficulty that would lead them to consider separation or even divorce. Now, however, things are different. Today they don't speak about joy, but about the many ways they have been hurt. They don't speak about how wonderful their partner makes them feel; instead, they discuss the troublesome elements of their relationship. You might say that these couples have years of relationship trash all over their home. Their house isn't full of old newspapers, empty milk jugs, or rotten banana peels, but it is full of memories of hurt, destruction, and discouragement. They each feel as if they are walking on eggshells under a dark cloud of despair. They have made a huge mess and they feel like prisoners in their own home.

How did this happen? How did these couples move from where you are (happy and excited) to where they are (upset and disappointed)? Often the answer comes down to problem solving. This chapter will help you take out the relationship trash every day so that you are never in the same position as these counselees. The Lord provides a much better way than hoarding relationship pain all over your house. Learning to problem-solve is one key way to enjoy marriage as God intended.

Understanding what the Bible says on this subject is important because of the ways our culture has lied to us about the issue of problem solving.

Lie #1: We Won't Have Any Problems, so Why Worry about This Topic?

I realize that you and your fiancé(e) are probably having a wonderful time together. In fact, you may be going through this book only because your church requires it! You don't actually have any problems.

I am thrilled that the two of you are enjoying life and that you are ready to commit to loving each other for the rest of your lives. I am not trying to be mean, but please remember this: Before you get married, you are putting your best foot forward. Your hair is done, your deodorant is working, and you want to spend the time together. In other words, you are together at times that are convenient for both of you. When you get married, your spouse will be there in your best moments—and in your worst. Your spouse will be there when you want to be alone. Your mate will want to talk when you want to sleep. He or she will complain about something when you are already irritated about work. What happens then?

There's no question that marriage can be wonderful and we want it to be all that God intends. But you *will* have problems. There *will* be times when Jesus is not at the center of your life as a couple. Someone once said that no relationship can last over the long term unless you learn to solve problems. You would be wise to take this chapter particularly seriously.

Lie #2: It's Easier to Ignore Problems than It Is to Solve Them

A second lie that many couples believe is that ignoring problems is easier than solving them. In the short term, it sure seems like it. Let's say Kerry makes what she thinks is a wonderful dinner for her husband Ben. Kerry researched popular cooking websites and found a great recipe. She bought the extra ingredients she needed and she was very excited to serve Ben the new dish. The problem is that Ben had a hard day at work and on days like that, he enjoys eating one of his favorites, Chicken Alfredo. When Ben arrives home, Kerry serves him the new dish it took her several hours to make. Ben thinks to himself, "I am not into adventure today. I had plenty of adventure at work. Now I want to eat something I know I will like." Ben does his duty and eats a small portion, but it is obvious that he doesn't like it. Kerry is hurt. She is angry. They give each other the silent treatment for the rest of the evening since neither really knows what to say. A few hours later, they go to bed. The next day is a new day and both essentially pretend that nothing happened.

It is unlikely that one disappointing meal will result in full-scale crisis, but it establishes a very important pattern for how Ben and Kerry handle problems. Figuratively speaking, Ben and Kerry wadded up a piece of paper and threw it on the floor as relationship trash. Ben hurt Kerry because he did not consider the time and energy she put into planning the meal and pleasing him. When a meal fails, the one who invested the effort is usually the one most upset. Rather than thanking Kerry and moving toward her graciously, Ben moved away. If the wound in Kerry's heart is not dealt with, it could fester into something worse. Without realizing it, Ben and Kerry slowly but surely are beginning a pattern that could ruin their relationship.

I could have just as easily discussed a situation involving in-law expectations, finances, an unsatisfactory sexual experience, or an unhelpful conversation. In any of these situations, learning to ignore problems is not only dangerous, it is not what Jesus wants a marriage to be.

Lie #3: It Is Easier to Wait until Problems Are Big Before You Worry about Them

Some things are more important than others. No doubt about that. However, that does not mean that things are insignificant. Some couples start out their marriage thinking that which direction the toilet paper goes, or who does the cleaning, or how clean the house needs to be for guests are minor deals. Indeed, they are right. However, minor deals can easily grow into big ones. When problems accumulate, there is more at stake. There has been more hurt and there are more examples of why it is unwise to trust the other person. There is more to confess. The more problems pile up, the harder they are to handle. This is because the couple has not learned to handle smaller problems as they come up. After all, it is very difficult to solve a complicated calculus problem if one has not completed algebra.

The problems you are facing today are probably relatively minor. Learning how to deal with them quickly will help you keep problems small and prepare you for the day you must face a more serious issue. Remember, problems are like bunnies. You can have two today and a thousand tomorrow!

If those are the lies we are susceptible to in our society, how can we solve problems with Jesus at the center?

Principle 1: You Must Take Responsibility for Your Part of the Problem

> "Why do you see the speck that is in your brother's eye, but do not notice the log that is in your own eye? Or how can you say to your brother, 'Let me take the speck out of your eye,' when there is the log in your own eye? You hypocrite, first take the log out of your own eye,

and then you will see clearly to take the speck out of
your brother's eye." (Matthew 7:3–5)

This passage from Jesus's Sermon on the Mount presents three
key points:

1. Before you judge someone, realize that you have a log-sized
    flaw yourself.
2. As long as you have the log, you aren't in a position to
    evaluate specks in someone else.
3. Only when your logs have been removed are you able to
    discuss specks.

This is so counter to the way people think! It's much more
common to tell the story like this: "Go and remove the log in your
brother's eye, because it is clear that he is blind. Do this quickly
before he has a chance to evaluate *your* log and use the information against you." My counselees have said countless times, "The
destruction of this marriage is her fault," or "Please get through to
my husband because I have been trying for years to no avail."

The temptation is to believe that your issue is far less significant
than your spouse's. Even if you don't claim to be sinless, you claim
that the vast majority of the problem lies with the other person.

When Jesus is at the center of your life and your marriage, you
look at problems differently. You realize that you must humble yourself first and admit your own wrongdoing. The Lord wants you to
have the humility needed to admit that you have the log while your
fiancé(e) or spouse has a speck. In other words, the problem lies
first and foremost with you. The Lord also wants you to be humble
enough to know that as long as a log is in your eye, you aren't in a
position to evaluate specks in anyone else's life.

You might be wondering, "How can I have this level of humility—and do I even *want* to be this humble? Won't that make me too

vulnerable so that I'm blamed for everything?" This level of humility starts with remembering all that you learned in chapters 1 and 2. When you are in a conflict with someone, don't just react to that person. Start with your relationship with Jesus: you and he both know that you are not free from sins and flaws. Yet he loved you despite them, and died to save you from them. He forgives your sin and he can set you free from the damage it does in your life. Your relationship with Christ is secure, so you can be humble (and grateful) enough to admit your faults to him. If you don't need to be defensive and self-righteous with God, it sets you free to be humble and honest with others, even in the middle of a conflict. When you model repentance yourself, and offer grace and mercy to your spouse with a 1 Corinthians 13 kind of love, it changes the dynamics of the conflict. It helps the other person to drop his or her defenses, pride, and judgmental spirit, and sets the stage for him or her to respond kindly as well. When you are standing before the Lord together, it enables you to face the problem honestly, humbly and with love, with a desire to please the Lord as you seek a solution.

Let's make this really practical. One day an engaged couple was registering at a local department store. How awesome is that? It's not every day that you are given a scanner and told to choose any item you want. This is Christmas on steroids! But in the midst of this fun activity, the couple began arguing about the color of the sheets they were going to scan. Admittedly, they were not going to call off the wedding over such a disagreement, but it was clear that he wanted one thing and she wanted another. These desires resulted in a significant conflict.

As I talked with them, my concern was not the conflict *per se*. My concern was how each person contributed to the argument. Each person needed to evaluate his or her own motives. They both needed to think about how they chose to place something at the center of their life besides Christ. Each one needed to see that, while the color of the sheets was not particularly important, how they related to each other and to God in the midst of the disagreement was very important. It set a pattern for the way they would handle issues in their marriage. In other words, both had to be willing to acknowledge that there was trash in the house. I'm happy to say that, as we talked about the situation, both the man and woman were able to remember the truths in chapters 1 and 2 and respond with humility about their part in the argument.

Principle 2: You Must Repent for Your Part of the Problem

> As it is, I rejoice, not because you were grieved, but because you were grieved into repenting. For you felt a godly grief, so that you suffered no loss through us. For godly grief produces a repentance that leads to salvation without regret, whereas worldly grief produces death. (2 Corinthians 7:9–10)

Once each person is willing to consider how he or she contributed to a particular struggle, they are ready to move to the second step of the process. That is, they are ready to pick up the trash. To pick up the trash, each person must repent.

To repent is to turn, to go in the other direction. This is probably the most difficult part of the process, because it is here that you admit that something is your fault. In the case of the couple who argued about the sheets, each person would have to repent of their anger, frustration, and language toward the other. They would have to admit that their desire to convince the other person went far beyond what the Lord would have wanted. They could admit that there was no willingness to compromise (why not list both colors?). It is important to not only repent of the action, but to acknowledge that your heart wanted the wrong thing as well.

Individuals and couples who face their own hearts and sinful responses are in the best place to build happy marriages. How are they able to do this? By believing that Jesus provides all they truly need. They are so secure in the grace of Jesus that they are able to confess and repent to each other.

Principle 3: You Must Forgive One Another

Then Peter came up and said to him, "Lord, how often will my brother sin against me, and I forgive him? As many as seven times?" Jesus said to him, "I do not say to you seven times, but seventy-seven times.

"Therefore the kingdom of heaven may be compared to a king who wished to settle accounts with his servants. When he began to settle, one was brought to him who owed him ten thousand talents. And since he could not pay, his master ordered him to be sold, with his wife and children and all that he had, and payment to be made. So the servant fell on his knees, imploring him, 'Have patience with me, and I will pay you everything.' And out of pity for him, the master of that servant released him and forgave him the debt. But when that same servant went out, he found one of his fellow servants who owed him a hundred denarii, and seizing him, he began to choke him, saying, 'Pay what you owe.' So his fellow servant fell down and pleaded with him, 'Have patience with me, and I will pay you.' He refused and went and put him in prison until he should pay the debt. When his fellow servants saw what had taken place, they were greatly distressed, and they went and reported to their master all that had taken place. Then his master summoned him and said to him, 'You wicked servant! I forgave you all

that debt because you pleaded with me. And should
not you have had mercy on your fellow servant, as I
had mercy on you?' And in anger his master delivered
him to the jailers, until he should pay all his debt. So
also my heavenly Father will do to every one of you,
if you do not forgive your brother from your heart."
(Matthew 18:21–35)

This is where you take the trash out to the street, where you can
see that the problem is resolved. Let's make a few observations from
this passage.

First, you can see that forgiveness is required all the time. Jesus
was not interested in a person counting to 490. He was interested in
his followers forgiving all the time. This does not mean that you will
always feel like forgiving. The Lord often encourages us to do what
is right even if we are struggling to do it. He knows what our hearts
need. If a person is unwilling to forgive, he will function just like a
hoarder. He will store up in his mind relationship hurts, pains, and
struggles and dwell on them. It is a recipe for disaster.

Second, Jesus chooses to tell a story with a number of crucial
contrasts to drive home the point. The first servant owes 10,000 talents (an enormous amount, given that only 3,000 talents of gold
were used to construct the temple) while the other servant owes
100 denarii (a day's wage for a common laborer). The first servant
is "brought to the king" while the second servant is "choked." Both
servants plead for mercy, but only one receives it. Jesus intends
his followers to understand that each character in the story represents someone in real life. The king is God, the first servant is you,
and the second servant is a person who has created a relationship
debt with you. In many cases, people struggle to forgive because
they compare the amount of forgiveness they have received from
their spouse to the amount they have given their spouse. But when
people compare the forgiveness God has given them in Christ to the

forgiveness they have given others, they see just how much more they have been forgiven. This passage shows us that there is no way we can ever out-forgive God. It simply is not possible. There are not enough 100 denarii debts to make up the 10,000 talents. The gospel changes how we look at our own faults and how we look at the faults of others. It makes us more willing to forgive.

Third, it is helpful to consider more carefully what this forgiveness would look like in real life. Let's say that Joe and Susan are two months from their wedding. They sent out "save the date" cards when they were first engaged, but now they must choose the invitations. Susan and her mom looked at various options but, due to either cost or style, they decided to go with a handmade version. Susan and her mom worked on a design, with the final touch being a bead on the invitation. Joe did not seem interested in the invitations until Susan showed him the final version. Joe was not enthused at all and essentially said that they were ugly and better cards were available at Walmart. Susan could not believe her ears. She oscillated between anger and hurt. An intense argument followed, with hurt feelings on both sides.

What should they do about this? Well, Joe would have been much better off to let Susan and her mom handle the invitations and spend time doing something more productive (which would have been basically anything!). But since this happened, they have to deal with it.

Joe must take responsibility for the way he handled this situation. He should ask for Susan's forgiveness for being uninterested during the design process and then inconsiderate in his response to the final product. He may also need to repent for his response to Susan when she got angry with him. Susan certainly has no fault regarding the invitations, but she may not have responded in a godly way to Joe's criticism. She may not be at fault in the initial confrontation, but she may have a share of responsibility for the argument that followed.

In short, real repentance and real forgiveness are needed in both directions. Forgiveness includes three practical steps:

1. The person promises not to bring up the incident up to the detriment of the other person.

This doesn't mean that the incident can never be discussed again. However, it means that the person will not use it as evidence to harm the other. In this case, when Susan forgave Joe, she promised not to use this incident to put him down or improve her own position in the relationship.

2. The person promises not to talk about it with others.

Love covers sin; that is to say, love hides sin. Instead of broadcasting the sins of other people, love keeps the circle of knowledge as small as possible. Susan is not going to talk about Joe's insensitivity to her girlfriends.

3. The person promises not to dwell on it.

In forgiving Joe, Susan is also promising that she will not spend her mental energy replaying the scenario over and over in her mind and getting upset at him all over again. She will choose not to focus on his sin in her thoughts. I think this is the most difficult commitment to make. It refers to the ongoing willingness of one person to treat the other person with kindness and love even when she has been hurt.

Principle 4: You Must Move Forward

> Brothers, I do not consider that I have made it my own. But one thing I do: forgetting what lies behind and straining forward to what lies ahead, I press on toward the goal for the prize of the upward call of God in Christ Jesus. (Philippians 3:13–14)

This is one of my favorite Bible passages. So many people seem to live in the past, haunted by their past failures and struggles. This passage says that you are free to move past it. Once you have repented and been forgiven, it is time to embrace the forgiveness. Trust me, you are not worthy of forgiveness, but we have a Savior who is amazingly forgiving. When that forgiveness comes, we are free!

The formula sounds so easy. On the one hand, it really is. If Jesus is the center of your life, you know it is only by God's grace that you are able to take out the trash and move forward in an honest and healing way. God's grace is so strong that you are able to resolve both little and big conflicts as they occur in your lives. This not only results in a strong and lasting marriage but one that honors the Lord and enjoys all the blessings God intended.

Homework Discussion Questions

Complete the following questions on your own and share your answers with your fiancé(e). Later, discuss your answers and your conversation as a couple with your mentor.

Think deeply about these questions. Shallow answers will hurt you and your future spouse more than anyone else. Deeper, more honest answers may lead to some uncomfortable moments, but that is okay. These real-life discussions will help you prepare and learn as a couple.

Choose a married couple you know well (possibly parents) and evaluate how you have seen them handle problems. Do they take responsibility, repent, forgive, and move forward? Do they ignore problems?

1. On a scale of 1–10, rate how biblical you have been in your problem solving. Why do you think you have not been

more biblical in your approach? What do you think is the first step toward being more biblical?

2. Be ready to share with your mentor two problems that you have had in your relationship. Carefully evaluate what you needed to take responsibility for. Did you repent and forgive or did you just seek to move forward? What do you need to do differently next time?

3. What two statements in this chapter had the most impact on you? What was it about those statements that struck you? Be prepared to discuss this with each other and with your mentor.

4. Skim this chapter again and look for the Bible passage most significant to you. Put it on an index card and review it each day until your appointment with your mentor. At this point you should have three index cards, one for each chapter.

5. What have you learned about Christ that would help you in biblically solving problems?

6. Why do you think a meaningful relationship with Jesus is so important to solving problems the way this chapter suggests?

7. Record any arguments or problems you have in the coming week and how you choose to handle them. If you do not have a conflict, choose a past one and think it through with your mentor.

8. Spend at least five minutes daily praying for yourself and your future spouse, that Jesus would truly be the center of your life and that your love for each other would be biblical.

Advanced Homework

Here are two additional homework possibilities that you as a couple may find helpful:

1. Read the book of Judges. Many people have taught that there is a cycle in Judges: sin, repentance, and rescue. However, if you read more carefully, you discover that you never see the word "repent," nor do you see deeds of repentance. The pattern is more like: sin, whine about it, and rescue. Judges illustrates two very important points: (1) The people never developed a heart for God and suffered immensely for it, and (2) God is so gracious that he often delivered them anyway. Imagine the blessings God would have given if they had been willing to put him at the center of their lives.

2. Read *From Forgiven to Forgiving* by Jay Adams (Amityville, NY: Calvary Press, 1994). This short book on forgiveness is the perfect antidote for relational hoarding. Remembering that Jesus has forgiven you changes everything.

Chapter 4

Roles and Expectations with Jesus as the Center

ALL OF US grew up in homes where we saw and experienced the way our parents functioned. For most of us, there were some good things and some not-so-helpful ones. Our reactions to those experiences shape our attitudes about what to expect when we marry and establish our own home. For example, you (the future husband) may have grown up in a home where your mother did most of the cleaning, the cooking, the laundry, and the homework with the children. Your father worked outside the home and handled the finances, legal matters, and vehicle maintenance. That's how your parents made it work; at least that's how it appeared to you. If your response to that environment is positive, you will probably desire something similar for your own home. But this set of expectations may not fit the expectations of your future bride.

She may have grown up in a home where her father took advantage of her mother and ultimately divorced her. Your fiancée may be sensitive about the need to ensure her own security because she saw her mom suffer so much. She would like to work outside the home, with a much more even split of household duties.

Each of us has learned a system for how relationships do or do not work. The Lord allowed those elements to be part of our story and they cannot be ignored. However, those elements of our story are not determinative. We don't have to assume that either adopting our parents' methods or rejecting them will automatically help us create a strong and lasting marriage. That's why it is important to go back to the Bible. As we develop our understanding of how each person is to function in the marriage, let's begin by understanding how the Lord, the Designer of marriage, knew it would work best. When we understand the Lord's perspective, we can use it to consider how the two of you can approach different aspects of your relationship.

God designed marriage with some elements that are nonnegotiable and other elements in which he gives us complete freedom. In the nonnegotiable areas, it is fascinating to notice that Jesus serves as the ultimate example. That is why it is so important to have Jesus at the center of your lives.

Let's think first about the roles God has given to the husband. These are nonnegotiables.

God's Expectations for a Biblical Husband

The husband's responsibilities are enormous but not onerous. They will require constant dependence on Christ, constant reflection on biblical and gospel truth, and a willingness to walk in humility. But what they lead to is freedom, enjoyment, and a life that is protected from the constant pressures of the world. These expectations can be described with three simple words, all beginning with the letter "L."

Lover

Husbands, love your wives, as Christ loved the church and gave himself up for her, that he might sanctify her, having cleansed her by the washing of water with the word, so that he might present the church to himself in splendor, without spot or wrinkle or any such thing, that she might be holy and without blemish. In the same way husbands should love their wives as their own bodies. He who loves his wife loves himself. For no one ever hated his own flesh, but nourishes and cherishes it, just as Christ does the church, because we are members of his body. "Therefore a man shall leave his father and mother and hold fast to his wife, and the two shall become one flesh." This mystery is profound, and I am saying that it refers to Christ and the church. However, let each one of you love his wife as himself, and let the wife see that she respects her husband. (Ephesians 5:25–33)

This is clearly the most challenging expectation. In chapter 2 we considered the real definition of biblical love. We had to face the reality that some folks get married because the other person helps them love themselves better than anyone else. But Ephesians 5 includes several additional observations that are helpful.

First, the command to love is given three times in just a few verses. Apparently, men, we need to hear this command more than once! Loving someone with biblical love is not easy. It is choosing to give, serve, care, provide, and protect someone else even when suffering comes from her hand. Lord willing, your marriage won't include many moments when you must love in the face of harsh treatment. However, anyone who has been married for any length of time will confess that there are moments when love must reign where retaliation would be more natural.

Second, the command to love is compared to the love Jesus has for his church. That love is described as giving, sanctifying, and presenting perfect in Ephesians 5. Jesus's love for the church cost him dearly. He was rejected, betrayed, and crucified by the people he loved. He felt the wrath of God because he loved them. The Bible calls husbands to love their wives as Jesus loved the church. This is not only a lifelong process, it is a task that requires the ongoing work of God in our own hearts. That work includes the Holy Spirit reminding us of the great truths we studied in chapter 1. (Romans 8:31–35 may even be on one of your index cards.) Being reminded that Jesus prays for us, keeps his promises to us, and never leaves us or forsakes us provides the strength we need to love our wives as Jesus loves his church. It is a task that requires humility when pride clamors for control.

Third, the text assumes that you already love yourself enough. Our culture talks a lot about the importance of loving ourselves. After all, it says, we are only able to love others if we love ourselves. Yet the overwhelming testimony of Scripture is that you love yourself enough as it is. Remember our earlier comments that many people get married not because they love the other person, but because the other person helps them love *themselves* better than anyone else does? That is not the biblical pattern or goal. Scripture places the emphasis on loving others.

Husbands, this calling is enormous. It will impact the way you treat your wife when you come home from work. Will you serve her or expect her to serve you? It will impact how you talk about her with others. Will you "present her perfect" in public or will you talk about her faults and failures? Your willingness to love will be revealed when you want something that she doesn't want. Maybe you want to go hunting, maybe you want to hang out with your buddies, or maybe you want sex. Will biblical love be your default mode or will self-love rule in those moments?

Is it easy to fulfill this calling? Of course not! But that is one more illustration of the significance of Christ's love, care, compassion, and grace to you. You can choose to love because Christ chose to love you; you can confess your selfishness and rely on him for the love you need for your wife. You can choose to give because

Christ chose to give his life for you, and he continues to give you everything you need to enjoy God and glorify him (Philippians 1:6). Marriage is about the worship of Christ and our dependence on him. It is the only way we can love our wives like Christ loves the church. That is why Jesus must be at the center.

Learner

> Likewise, husbands, live with your wives in an
> understanding way, showing honor to the woman as
> the weaker vessel, since they are heirs with you of the
> grace of life, so that your prayers may not be hindered.
> (1 Peter 3:7)

Four elements in this verse are particularly significant for our purposes. First, husbands are to live with their wives in an understanding way or "according to knowledge." This is where the learner concept comes in. God commands husbands to pay particular attention to their wives. Notice that the call is not to understand women in general. The call is to understand the woman you are going to marry. This will mean that a husband invests the time and energy it takes to understand his wife.

I will never forget my first lesson on this subject. My wife and I had been married for less than a year. We were young; we had no children and very little responsibility outside of work. We had dinner together most evenings and normally had a few hours each night to be together. One Friday morning my wife said, "I am looking forward to this weekend when we can spend time together." I thought I had married a crazy woman! We spent time together every single evening! How was this weekend going to be different? What I later learned was that my definition of spending time together and her definition were not entirely the same. I thought if you both were in the same place at the same time, you were spending time together. She defined time together in a much more restrictive sense. We needed to be relating emotionally. We needed to be looking into each other's eyes. We needed to give each other undivided attention. I had no idea that spending time together was so complicated! When you get married, there will be many "little things" that you will need to learn as well.

Second, husbands are expected to show their wives honor. Now that I have been married over twenty years, I think I understand that more than I once did. Let's face it, both of you have dirty laundry. But showing honor means that our dirty laundry stays hidden in the closet. Rather than broadcast faults, irritations, or areas of immaturity to others, a godly husband will choose to handle those matters behind closed doors.

In addition, honoring involves valuing the commitment that your fiancée is about to make to you. In the book of Malachi, we find a very interesting comment. The Lord is upset with his people because the men were divorcing their wives. As one reads the text, it becomes apparent that the men had lived with their wives during their best years—years when they were the most physically attractive, energetic, and most likely to produce children. In other words, the women had given their husbands their very best years. The husbands responded by divorcing their wives once those years were past. In God's mind, that was (and is) very wicked. Honoring requires you to treat your wife with excellence all the days of her life. I would add that honoring is not simply refusing to broadcast her faults; it also involves sharing the many ways she is a blessing to you. Honoring hides what is negative and shares what is positive.

Third, verse 7 concludes with the sobering words, "so that your prayers will not be hindered." God says that there is a sense in which he will not listen to our prayers if we are not concerned to understand and honor our wives. Very rarely in the Bible do we find God telling his people that he will not listen to them. Men, please take these words seriously. I think some men forget that their wife is also the Lord's child. No father, and certainly not the heavenly Father, wants to see one of his daughters mistreated. So men, please see the seriousness of this command. The most important lifeline in your marriage is your communion with God. If that lifeline is not active, you and your family will suffer.

Fourth and finally, notice "in the same way" in the text. This requires us to ask, "The same way as what?" As we consider the context, we see the same phrase in 1 Peter 3:1. Apparently, "in the same way" has its meaning even earlier in the book. At the end of chapter 2, we see that Christ is our example—in "entrusting himself to God." You see, men, fulfilling the commitment to be a learner isn't easy. It is hard work. How can you accomplish that amid your other responsibilities? The answer is to follow in the footsteps of Jesus Christ and entrust yourself to God. Sometimes we men want peace, quiet, and relaxation after we come home from work. Yet the command to live with our wives in an understanding way is often at odds with what we want. But isn't that the example of Jesus? In the garden of Gethsemane he prayed, "Not my will, but yours, be done" (Luke 22:42). He understood what was ahead for him and he was not looking forward to it. Yet he believed that God would give him the strength to do what he was called to do. It is the same with us. Let's be husbands that entrust ourselves to the plan and will of God by choosing to give our wives our time, attention, and focus. You will have to set aside your agenda to follow Christ. Jesus told his followers that they had to take up their cross daily (die to their own wants) and follow him (Luke 9:23). However, I can promise you that setting aside your agenda will result in great blessing.

Leader

Men were designed to lead, particularly in marriage and in the church. But these days leadership is either made fun of and dismissed or confused with dictatorship. Biblical leadership functions differently. Jesus taught on leadership in Matthew 20.

But Jesus called them to him and said, "You know that the rulers of the Gentiles lord it over them, and their great ones exercise authority over them. It shall not be so among you. But whoever would be great among you must be your servant, and whoever would be first among you must be your slave, even as the Son of Man came not to be served but to serve, and to give his life as a ransom for many." (Matthew 20:25–28)

The picture Jesus paints is one of servant leadership, not the portrait of a dictator. I realize that there are a few times in life where some hard decisions have to be made. But that does not mean men need to act like Gentile lords in the process. Here are two very early examples in my own marriage where leadership was required.

My wife Stephanie was in nursing school when we married. She felt a lot of pressure to be a wife and student while working a part-time job. I was finishing my undergraduate degree and working a couple of part-time jobs myself. It was clear just three months into our marriage that Stephanie's load was too heavy at that point in her life. As we talked about the situation, we learned she had three distinct roles: wife, student, worker. I made the decision that she needed to quit work. After all, her wife role wasn't changing and she honestly believed that God had opened the door for nursing school. If God wanted her to be a wife and a student, the only thing left was her part-time job. Initially she protested, fearing that we would be homeless. I promised her that I would do whatever I needed to in order for us to survive, but that her job was over. This may sound a bit dictatorial, but in reality it was servant leadership. I took full responsibility for our finances and she was set free from one source of pressure in her life. She now admits that my decision was one of the most loving acts I did for her in the first few years of our marriage. It proved to her that I had her interests in mind and not simply my own.

A few months later, a very different situation arose. I finished my degree and I had multiple job offers with very different pros and cons for each job. I admitted to Stephanie that I did not think I could see clearly enough to make a wise decision. I seemed to change my mind every few hours. It was clear that I needed guidance. While I had asked her opinion many times, the time was nearing when a decision had to be made. I asked her which job she wanted me to take. I promised that I would not fuss about it, I would not blame her for anything that went wrong, and I promised that we would work together on whatever option we picked. In the sovereignty of God, she was able to see the big picture better than I could. We went with her option and it turned out that she was exactly right. I still viewed the choice as our choice and I knew that it was my job to lead us in making our decision successful. However, I also had to recognize that my heart was at war and I was losing the battle for wisdom. God gave Stephanie the ability to look at both companies and the pros and cons of both jobs and that made the difference in making the right choice. Making a decision this way required a fair bit of humility on my part. I had to admit my struggles and allow her skills, abilities, and wisdom to make up for my deficiencies. But leadership on my part also meant that I could not blame her during any challenging days that followed.

This style of servant leadership does not come naturally. Since it is based on the example of Christ, it will require Christ to be at the center of your life. Worship directed to anything other than the Lord will make servant leadership very difficult, if not impossible.

It is my prayer that you as the man would commit yourself, before the Lord and your fiancée, to do this in humble reliance on God's grace. It is my prayer that you will be flexible on all your expectations, but rigid on God's design. I pray that you will have fifty-five years (or more!) of marriage as God intended for his glory, and that you will set aside all power trips, all self-righteousness, and all self-pity for the goal of a marriage that represents Christ.

Biblical Role of a Wife

Just as the Lord gave instructions to husbands, he also gives instructions for wives. It is helpful to remember that what follows does not apply to all relationships. I believe there is a general principle regarding the roles of men and women in society, but there is no question that our discussion is particularly geared toward husbands and wives. Thus, the commitments discussed here apply to marriage relationships specifically and do not fully apply during the engagement period. Nevertheless, it is very important for a woman to wholeheartedly believe that she can make these commitments to her fiancé without reservation. As I did with the role of the husband, let's use three words to describe the role of a wife.

Follower

Wives are commanded to submit to their husbands. There is no doubt that this commitment is a bit scary. Reading these passages makes that fear very real. God is very clear about his expectations and there is very little wiggle room around his commandments. You are willfully choosing to relate to your husband differently than you will relate to anyone else. You are accepting him as your lifelong leader and authority. Notice what the Bible says:

> Wives, submit to your own husbands, as to the Lord. (Ephesians 5:22)

> Likewise, wives, be subject to your own husbands, so that even if some do not obey the word, they may be won without a word by the conduct of their wives, when they see your respectful and pure conduct. Do not let your adorning be external—the braiding of hair and the putting on of gold jewelry, or the clothing you wear—but let your adorning be the hidden person of the

heart with the imperishable beauty of a gentle and quiet spirit, which in God's sight is very precious. For this is how the holy women who hoped in God used to adorn themselves, by submitting to their own husbands, as Sarah obeyed Abraham, calling him lord. And you are her children, if you do good and do not fear anything that is frightening. (1 Peter 3:1–6)

Being a follower does not mean that your opinion is unimportant or that you are less important in the marriage. It simply means that God has ordained one person to ride on the front seat of the tandem bike and the other to ride on the back. The bike will, of course, move fastest when both people are peddling together, so unison and teamwork should characterize your marriage overall.

The two of you will agree on a great many things; there should be many times in your marriage where you are simply together. However, a follower is put to the test when the leader makes a choice different from what the follower desires. If you (as a wife) believe your husband is leading you in an unhelpful way, you may be tempted to quit peddling, thinking to yourself, "Fine, if you want to go in that direction, you will do it yourself." Worse, you might be tempted to jump off the bike entirely, refusing to go with him. Being a follower means that unless your husband is directly leading you to sin, you will choose to continue peddling even if you would make a different decision. Thus, in the days ahead, remember that being a follower when you are getting what you want is easy. The challenge in obeying these commands occurs when your husband is leading in a way that you do not appreciate.

A woman might ask, "How is this possible? How can I entrust my life to a person who is free to make decisions even if I do not like them?" These are legitimate questions. The answer goes back to chapter 1: When Jesus is at the center of your life and your marriage, you can submit to your husband because you are trusting the

Lord to be at work in the situation. Not only can you submit, you can continue to peddle toward the destination.

Be prepared, your husband may fail in his leadership. In fact, it is highly likely that he will. That is okay. Failure is one way God helps all of us grow and see our need for continual dependence on Christ. In the long run, having a few failures will produce a more godly husband, a much better leader, and a much stronger union.

It is also helpful to remember that, while your husband may make a wrong leadership decision, that does not mean you are immune from foolishness yourself. There will be times when your choices would not have glorified God or built your marriage either. In those circumstances you can praise the Lord that he gave you a husband who was willing to exercise leadership and avert the consequences of your choices.

Submission is a hard subject and all of us struggle with it. But that does not mean submission is bad, unhealthy, or a hindrance to our walk with Christ.

It must be said that on occasion marriages become toxic. The husband is not trying to lead his family to a more meaningful relationship with Christ; rather, he is building his own little kingdom of oppression. While I hope and pray that your marriage never reaches that point, it is important to remember a couple of principles when facing such situations.

First, the husband is not the final authority. All of the husband's authority is delegated both by God and by his wife, who willingly took the position of submission. He is accountable to God and his wife for the way he exercises that authority. Husbands are wise to remember that God also established the authority of the church and the authority of government. In some circumstances, the authority given by God to the church and to government overrides the husband's authority. So there may be times when it is appropriate for a wife to involve both the civil authorities and the church leadership. Many churches are, thankfully, taking a much more aggressive stand against dictator husbands who create kingdoms of oppression.

Second, a wife is free to seek help from church leadership without her husband. If she has confronted him on a particular issue and he refuses to acknowledge her concerns or address them biblically, she has a right, given in Matthew 18:15–20, to request church leadership to evaluate the circumstances and judge accordingly. I do not believe that a couple seeking to put Jesus at the center of their marriage will ever need this advice, but if Jesus is not the center of your life and if the gospel is not something you think about on a regular basis, then anything is possible. The point is that a wife's submission cannot be a tool her husband uses to sinfully oppress her.

Companion

> Therefore a man shall leave his father and his mother
> and hold fast to his wife, and they shall become one
> flesh. (Genesis 2:24)

Genesis 2:24 teaches the importance of being a companion to your husband (and he to you). God said, "It is not good for the man to be alone." While single individuals often occupy important places in the Bible, Jesus himself above all, even Paul as a single man cites Genesis 2:24 three different times. The Bible views marriage as a solution to being alone. In God's world there is something powerful about navigating through life with a companion. We saw earlier that marriage is an institution established by God for his glory and our blessing. Even when sin entered the world, the blessing of marriage remained. God in his grace did not want you to have to celebrate victories and blessings alone. In addition, life in a broken world is sometimes very difficult. Losing a job, having a house fire, being in a serious accident, experiencing poor health, or losing a child are incredibly painful experiences. The Lord's presence is always our most important source of joy and strength, but he also designed the companionship of marriage to be a source of comfort and encouragement through life's challenges. As you approach your own marriage, you want to develop a heart that says, "We are in this together. There may be some very rough waters, but we will always navigate them together."

Your companionship is not just physical. To experience the full depth of relationship, you should seek to enjoy your husband emotionally, spiritually, and physically. The more you relate at each of these levels, the stronger your bond will become. As you grow together, you should expect to mature emotionally. This means that biblical thinking will control your emotions. Your spiritual connection should grow as you watch the Lord work in each other's lives through the years. Your physical bond should also strengthen as you become more and more comfortable with each other.

Second, notice that Genesis 2:24 says that a woman is to leave her father and mother, just as the man is to leave his. This sounds really harsh. But God's point is that your most important human relationship moves from your parents and your childhood home to your husband and the new home you are establishing with him. Your position is changing. You may have had twenty-plus years of parental care and nurture; it can be difficult to trust yourself to a man who has a lot of proving to do. But continuing to run to your parents does not honor God. True, your husband should be patient as the ties are slowly cut with your parents and replaced with ties to him.[1] But do not miss the fact that God expects you to develop new ties with your husband.

---

1. My wife was about to turn twenty-two when we married. When she turns forty-four it will be official—I will have officially cared for her longer than her parents did. But in the first year or two, I had to recognize that my wife's desire to have her parents' approval was not a criticism of me; it was a statement of trust for two people who loved her, cared for her, and tried to put her in the best possible position for adult life. She needed to "leave," but I needed to acknowledge that her parents had a much longer track record than I had. In time, my care made it easier for her to "leave."

Respect

> However, let each one of you love his wife as himself,
> and let the wife see that she respects her husband.
> (Ephesians 5:33)

A third word that summarizes the role God gives a wife is "respect." Ephesians 5:33 is actually a summary of all that God says in verses 22–33, so what the Lord wrote about wives in this passage is captured by the term "respect." When you couple this with Colossians 3:9, a pattern emerges. Some women irritate their husbands, making it easy for them to become bitter against them. This does not excuse husbands' bitterness, but it demonstrates the power that wives have in their husbands' lives. There are many ways that a wife can respect her husband, but here are three ideas.

First, a wife can respect her husband by recognizing all the ways that he is a blessing to her. It is amazing how much changes when our thinking changes. Maybe that is why the Lord encouraged us in Philippians 4:8–9 to think on those things that are true, lovely, and ultimately the things that are excellent. What you choose to dwell upon regarding your husband will greatly impact how you see him. If you choose to focus on his failures (and he, like all of us, will have plenty of them), you will find him frustrating, irritating, and annoying. You may even consider him an obstacle to the things you hope to accomplish. But if you look at him through the lens of the ways he is blessing you, you will see him as a gracious gift of God designed, in part, to enrich your life. You will love him because he treats you with kindness, gentleness, and care.

Second, a wife can respect her husband by refusing to say, "I told you so." There will be many times in your marriage when you are right. Just because he has the position of leader does not always mean he makes the right decisions. Sometimes he will do things that are just plain stupid and you will pay the price for it. But that does not mean you have to remind him of it. Unless your husband becomes a very self-centered man, he will not be proud of his mistakes. In fact, he will feel ashamed and embarrassed by them. This shame and embarrassment should lead to his genuine repentance, as opposed to a worldly sorrow that produces no good fruit (2 Corinthians 7:10). However, assuming your future husband wants to live for the Lord, one way to encourage him to continue leading is not to make a point about how foolish he is.

Third, a wife can respect her husband by encouraging his areas of success. I know that some women don't appreciate the cheerleader analogy, but it fits this point well. As wives, you are your husband's greatest supporter and encourager. When I was writing my Ph.D. dissertation, there were many days that I wanted to quit. Yet in each of those moments my wife was cheering me on, giving me time to work on my project, and celebrating every victory along the way. You will bless your husband if you find ways to celebrate his areas of success.

If you both commit to the roles God has assigned, you will experience joy in honoring the Lord in your marriage. Consider this: if you marry in your mid-twenties and live until eighty (about the average these days), you will have about fifty-five years together. The decisions you make about how you will fulfill your role and care for your spouse will impact the vast majority of your life. If you live according to God's design, your years together may have a few bumps in the road, but you can get through them together. Guard against the mentality that says, "I will do my role if you will do yours." If Jesus is the center of your life and your marriage, you will each want to live out your roles because it is a joy and honor to live for Christ.

Have you noticed that this discussion of roles in marriage leaves a lot of flexibility in how a household is run? Scripture does not say who must organize the daily finances or who does the laundry, the cooking, the cleaning, or the car maintenance. God has gifted each of you differently. What works for one couple will not necessarily be best for another. Each couple has to learn what works best, given each person's skills, gifts, abilities, and desires.

So let me encourage you to enjoy building a life together. Things may change over time, but if Jesus is at the center of your life, you can enjoy the process. What are nonnegotiable are God's expectations for how a husband and wife function. Jesus equips us through the Spirit to do what God has commanded. The requirements are lofty but not impossible. We are not able to fulfill them perfectly, of course, but that is what constantly drives us back to our need for the gospel, for humility, for forgiveness, for grace, and for the power of God. Jesus must be the center and you must be willing to commit the mental, physical, and spiritual energy to build your marriage relationship around him. Those who do will find great freedom and joy in their relationship.

Homework Discussion Questions

Complete the following questions on your own and then share your answers with your fiancé(e). Later, discuss your answers and your conversation as a couple with your mentor.

Be prepared think deeply about these questions. Shallow answers will hurt you and your future spouse more than anyone else. Deeper, more honest answers may lead to some uncomfortable moments, but that is okay. These real-life discussions will help you to prepare and learn as a couple.

1. Answer the following questions about yourself and discuss your answers with your fiancé(e):
   a. What are your three greatest fears about getting married?
   b. What do you do that irritates your future spouse?
   c. What two interests do you wish your fiancé(e) would share with you?

    d. What are three things you enjoy doing with your fiancé(e) at this stage of your relationship?

    e. What is the most important area in which you need to grow at this point?

2. Write out the five most important expectations you had for your future spouse before reading this chapter. Where did they come from? How important are they now?

3. To run a household, certain agreements need to be in place. Although there is a lot of flexibility, there still has to be a plan for laundry, shopping, managing the finances, cooking, cleaning, and yard work. What are your thoughts about how these duties will be accomplished? Be as specific as possible, but remember that things may change relatively early in your marriage.

4. Based on the answers to questions 2 and 3, where do you see potential for conflict?

5. Which two statements in this chapter had the most impact on you? What was it about them that particularly struck you?

6. Skim this chapter again and choose the Bible passage most significant to you. Write it on an index card and review it daily until your appointment with your mentor. You should now have four index cards—one for each chapter.

7. What truths have you learned about Christ that will help you in your role?

8. Write out how you believe your home will function when you get married, now that you have thought about roles and expectations.

9. Spend at least five minutes daily praying for yourself and each other, that Jesus would truly be the center of your life and that your love for each other would be biblical.

Advanced Homework

Here is an additional homework option that couples may find encouraging and beneficial:

- Read a book about your role as a husband or wife. (a) I recommend that men read *The Complete Husband* by Lou Priolo (Amityville, NY: Calvary Press, 1999). This book will challenge and encourage you to be a man who loves the Lord in his relationship with his wife. (b) I recommend that women read *Creative Counterpart* by Linda Dillow (Nashville: Thomas Nelson, 1986). If you love and serve your husband as she teaches, you will have one very blessed husband.

Chapter 5

Communication
with Jesus as the Center[2]

CONGRATULATIONS ON REACHING the halfway point in this book! Working through this material takes time and energy, but every hour you invest in this material before you are married will save you countless hours of struggle afterwards. Keep going—it is well worth it.

I hope it is clear that every aspect of our lives, including marriage, flows from our worship, love, and desire to honor Christ. One of the blessings of having Christ at the center of your life and marriage is that you can experience marriage as God intended it to be. Marriage is an institution that God designed for life on earth. It is meant to be one of our joys and pleasures. Only our own sin and selfishness corrupt what God designed to be so wonderful. I have watched people who have been married for forty, fifty, even seventy years (yes, seventy years of marriage!) love each other, care for each other, and make their way through life in joyful harmony. That can be true of you as well. Your marriage can be a source of great earthly joy. While that joy can never match the joy found in Jesus, it is one of the things that make life on earth fun and fulfilling.

---

2. This material is an adaptation from a minibook I wrote, entitled *Can We Talk?* (Greensboro, NC: New Growth Press, 2012).

Since marriage is designed to be an intimate relationship, it's not surprising that God's Word provides a lot of teaching about communication that can strengthen our marriages. As we seek to develop that kind of communication, it's not surprising that we will see once again that it has everything to do with Jesus being at the center of our lives and our relationship. Let's fast-forward a few years to consider a common communication struggle.

Bob turns out the lights on another day, a day just like yesterday. Home used to be the place he wanted to be, but not anymore. In fact, Bob often works late or looks for an excuse to stop somewhere—anywhere—on the way home. Julie, his wife, feels exactly the same way. Bob and Julie are frustrated that they cannot talk about anything significant without the conversation resulting in another argument. They argue about their children, their relationship, their money, and sometimes they just argue to argue. But this is not how Bob and Julie want their relationship to be. They love each other, they want to spend meaningful time together, and they want to communicate well. But it seems that the more time they spend together and the more they talk, the worse their relationship becomes. They feel trapped. They want to communicate well, but they just don't know how.

I think a lot of couples end up where Bob and Julie are. They never learn about healthy communication and over time their communication—and their relationship—slowly deteriorate. It doesn't have to be that way. There is hope to be found in Jesus Christ.

The Lord Jesus came to save us from our sins, to bring us into relationship with him, and to help us in the midst of our sin and our suffering. And God has given us his Word to direct our words and our lives.

Communication Begins with What You Want

Learning to communicate well is not just a matter of learning clearer ways to express yourself. You have to start where Jesus starts when he talks about our words—with what is going on inside you. It starts with looking at *why* we say the things we do. Jesus says that it is "out of the abundance of the heart the mouth speaks" (Matthew 12:34). What does he mean by that? In the Bible, the word "heart" is often used to describe our inner life—our thoughts and desires.

This is different from what we usually think, isn't it? How often have you thought or said something like, "I didn't think before I spoke," or "That's not what I meant to say." But Jesus is saying the opposite. He is saying that our main problem with our words is not that we speak without thinking, but that our words are expressing what's in our hearts! Our mouths can say only what has already been thought. The path of communication is from the inside out. The starting place for all communication (both good and bad) is the heart. That's why it isn't possible to make everything better simply through improved communication techniques. There are many couples (like Bob and Julie) who have learned new communication skills, but their relationship doesn't improve because there has been no change in what they wanted or desired.

If you want to communicate in a way that strengthens your relationships, you will need to think biblically about your heart, the control center for all that we are and do.

Communication Expresses What You Want

Everyone's speech flows from what they want or desire in a certain situation or relationship. Think about it: When you argue with your fiancé(e), aren't there things you want and aren't getting that are at work in that argument? When you speak kindly to your friend but criticize your neighbor, aren't there certain desires motivating your words? James 4:1–2 explains it like this:

> What causes quarrels and what causes fights among
> you? Is it not this, that your passions are at war within

> you? You desire and do not have, so you murder. You
> covet and cannot obtain, so you fight and quarrel. You
> do not have, because you do not ask. (James 4:1–2)

James says that our conflicts are not the result of an indifferent response from our fiancé(e), an annoying tone, or defensive body language (even though all those things are problematic). Instead, conflicts come from our desires, the same desires that are waging war inside us (v. 1). This truth is huge! It helps you understand something very important: conflicts occur because you want certain things. Notice how the text explained it: "you desire . . . so you murder." There it is: you want what you want, and you do what it takes to get it. Obviously, if you want one thing and your future spouse wants another, conflict is the inevitable result. Bob and Julie's desires resulted in communication (action), and the kind of communication they used resulted in arguments, frustration, and anger (consequences).

No communication struggle can properly be addressed without first dealing with the heart. We can be thankful that we have a Savior, Jesus, who encourages us to pray for help to repent of our selfish desires so that we will want to love God and love others. This is why Jesus must be the one we worship.

Let's return to Bob and Julie's struggle. As we examine the details of their situation, it can help us understand how what we want affects our communication.

What Bob Wants

I asked Bob to think about which of his wants and desires shape the way he communicates with Julie. As he did so, certain desires stood out. First, Bob often wanted Julie to agree with him. Obviously, spouses want agreement a good percentage of the time, but Bob discovered that he *demands* agreement from Julie. If Julie simply wants them to "agree to disagree," Bob gets upset and frustrated. This began before Bob and Julie married.

For example, as Bob and Julie discussed wedding plans, Bob had a small wedding in mind with very simple invitations. Julie was practically inviting everyone in the phone book. Bob wanted his wedding day to include people he loved and cared about. To him, it was not a day to pack a rental facility. Julie, however, paid $1200 for her wedding dress and was determined to have everyone see her in it. Bob finds this a bit absurd but Julie does not agree. So Bob spends ten minutes explaining the eight reasons why he is correct. Julie says she has had enough of the browbeating and the conversation ends with neither one very happy.

Bob's desire (for Julie to agree with his plan for a small wedding) led to division, separation, and frustration. This illustration may seem trivial, but it is played out regularly before a couple marries and intensifies afterwards. Do you see how a commitment to honor Christ in his relationship with Julie could have impacted Bob's motives at this point? Isn't it possible that, had he reflected on what would please the Lord (instead of what he wanted) and asked for the Spirit's help, things would have been radically different? Bob needed to understand that the conflict was not about the guest list; it was about his relationship with the Lord Jesus and his failure to love Julie sacrificially as Christ loves the church. When Bob's desires and demands led to division, separation, and frustration, his purpose changed from bringing glory to God to getting his way.

A second desire Bob identified was that he often wanted problems to be solved quickly. There had been signs of this during their engagement, but only later was the full manifestation of this desire evident. In Bob's mind, Julie wanted to talk about the same problems again and again without ever doing anything differently. Not only did these conversations drive Bob crazy, he disliked spending forty-five minutes discussing issues he considered trivial. Bob's desires directed his behavior. He was short-tempered. He did not pay close attention to Julie and often did not even look at her when she spoke. Why? Bob wanted the thirty-second version of the four problems for the day, and then he wanted to be done. Once again, Bob was really about Bob. He was not thinking about how Jesus loved him, or praying for the fruit of the Spirit to be present in these moments. He was not interested in helping Julie; he was interested in helping himself.

Can you see how the desires of Bob's heart have created an environment of tension and frustration? Can you see how very small issues (like a guest list or working on the wedding registry) become large issues and put a couple in a position where everyday conversation is difficult? Can you see that, without a change in Bob's heart, these desires will continue to result in strife and division? The point is that people's desires determine the words they use, their tone of voice, their attentiveness in conversation, and their body language. Unless self-centered desires are changed to focus on Jesus, asking him for forgiveness (for loving ourselves more than we love others) and help (to turn from what we want and consider what's best for our spouses), the communication problems will remain. Bob and Julie's conversation could have been radically redeemed if Bob's heart had been fixed on pleasing Jesus. But since communication failures are rarely a one-way street, let's turn our attention to Julie's desires.

What Julie Wants

As Julie evaluated their marriage, she realized that one of her major desires was to be heard. From her perspective, Bob did not seem to care about her opinion (maybe because he only wanted the thirty-second version!). It seemed that Bob just wanted to give an answer to a problem and move on to something else. Julie felt that Bob regularly ignored her and she reacted in frustration. Sometimes she cried to get Bob to look at her long enough for her to speak a few sentences. At other times, she fought back in anger. And sometimes she stopped communicating altogether. On one level, Julie can be applauded. She is trying to connect with Bob. She wants to engage him and talk things through. However, when Julie's desire to be heard becomes the most important thing to her, her communication becomes negative. When Julie does not find her identity and security in Christ, her relationship with Bob is impacted. When Bob's approval (instead of her desire to please Christ) become the most important thing in her life, that desire rules her inner life and affects the way she talks to Bob. She does not want to serve Bob, but to punish him through anger and resentment. There were signs of this before they got married, but the real fruit of this desire blossomed in the following years.

Also, when Bob gives Julie an opportunity to talk, Julie wants his undivided attention. The key word is *undivided.* When Bob tries to multitask while Julie is trying to talk to him (by going through the mail, cleaning up the kitchen, or reading the paper), she goes ballistic! Suddenly the living room is turned into a small-scale version of Mount St. Helens. Julie can't believe how insensitive and uncaring her husband is, especially since he made time for her during their engagement period. Once again, Julie is not totally wrong. Bob is being rude and insensitive. Julie should lovingly confront Bob about the way he treats her. However, when her desire for Bob's undivided attention becomes more important to her than loving him, then living out of God's love has taken second place in her heart. What has first place is getting what she wants from Bob and punishing him if he doesn't do as she demands.

The Scriptures teach that our talk reveals something we want deep down inside. Our words are an outflow of what is already present on the inside. This is where Bob and Julie need to focus. For their communication to improve, what they want has to change. They have to want to know and love Jesus more than they want their spouse to agree with them (quickly!), listen to them, and give them their full attention. They need to desire to please God with their responses. They need to repent and turn away from desires that have become too important and turn instead to Jesus.

In this case, Bob asked the Lord to forgive him for wanting Julie to agree with him and solve problems quickly *more than* he wanted to honor Jesus and love his wife. He asked Julie to forgive him for not loving her like Jesus loves the church. He committed himself to pleasing Christ above those other things. Julie asked God and Bob to forgive her for wanting to be heard and wanting Bob's undivided attention *more than* she wanted to please Jesus and love her husband. As a result, a wonderful thing happened in their marriage. For the first time, they realized why they kept having the same old arguments. They realized that there were things they wanted on the inside that were revealing themselves in ugly ways on the outside. What they wanted from each other was not wrong, but they saw that wanting anything more than loving God and each other was very wrong. Once they saw where they needed forgiveness, they could go to Jesus for forgiveness and help. Their communication struggles were not solved overnight, but these insights filled them with hope.

Use Bob and Julie's experience to help you think about any desires you have made more important than pleasing Jesus. What patterns do you see developing in the way you and your fiancé(e) relate? I'm sure that the two of you want to enjoy life together. I believe that it is possible to live together for decades and refuse to raise your voice in anger at each other, refuse to speak with the intent to injure each other, and instead to enjoy one another's company and conversations.

Both my wife and I remember being told, "You could sell tickets to your fights." We understood why the person said it. After all, Stephanie and I were both fairly intense people, and I'm sure the person had good intentions in warning us that our struggles could be electric. But ironically, this led Stephanie and me to realize that

God's Word did not say that we *had* to struggle. We would only struggle when our own hearts led us down that path. So we made a commitment to God and to each other not to argue—for one whole year. After that, all bets were off, of course! As we worked hard to keep our personal desires from rising above our desire to please Christ, we saw our relationship build harmony and closeness. I'm not saying that we never sinned, but when you looked at our relationship overall, it was not characterized by fights and quarrels. So we realized that we could continue to experience God's blessings as long as we remained dependent on him and focused on honoring him in our marriage. Now, by God's grace, over twenty years later, we are still able to work through our struggles without arguing or needing to learn how to "fight fair."

Take time now to answer these two very important questions:

1. What issues do you most commonly argue about with your fiancé(e) (e.g., finances, wedding planning, care of children)?

   a.

   b.

   c.

   d.

2. What underlying desires impact the way you discuss the issues you listed above (e.g., to have my opinion clearly heard)?

a.

b.

c.

d.

Jesus Wants Heart Change

My guess is that some of the desires you listed are not sinful in and of themselves. Instead, they are like Bob's or Julie's. You want to be heard, agreed with, and noticed. You want to solve problems as quickly as you can. But like Bob and Julie, perhaps you've begun to notice that it is not the desire itself that is sinful; it is how important the desire has become to you. A good desire becomes a sinful desire when it rules and controls your heart. Your heart is made to worship only one thing at a time, so you can't worship Jesus and still make what you want more important. It just won't work. That is why passages like 2 Corinthians 5:9 and 1 Corinthians 10:31 explain that pleasing Christ must be our most important priority.

How can you grow in wanting to please Christ? Start by remembering his kindness and mercy to you. Think back to the time when you first trusted Christ. He forgave you, removed your sin as far as the east is from the west, and gave you security for eternal life in heaven. His promises will never fail you; his strength is always available to you through the Holy Spirit. He will continue the good work he has begun in you until the day of his return (Philippians 1:6). Is it possible that you have lost sight of his love for you—and your love for him? Have you lost your first love (Revelation 2:4)? If you have, turn back to him. Ask him to forgive you and renew you, so that you can love him with all of your heart (Matthew 22:37–38).

Start your day by reminding yourself of what Christ has done for you. Spend time meditating on God's lovingkindness to you and your family. Search the Psalms and underline the phrases that describe what God has done for you. Write a list of all the things Jesus has forgiven you for. Spend time thinking about his sacrifice for you on the cross. Who else deserves first place in your desires and affections? It is the past, present, and future work of Jesus that should motivate you to love him and find joy in him. When you seek after God, you find him. When you beg him to help you grow in your love for him, he increases that love. Communication struggles start with the heart and so does communication redemption. Your sinful desires have already brought you heartache. But desire the Lord and you, like the psalmist, will "taste and see that the LORD is good" (Psalm 34:8). "Delight yourself in the LORD and he will give you the desires of your heart" (Psalm 37:4).

Jesus said in John 10:10–11, "The thief comes only to steal and kill and destroy. I came that they may have life and have it abundantly. I am the good shepherd. The good shepherd lays down his life for the sheep." Abundant life! Jesus did not say that you would merely tolerate life, slog through life, or survive life. He said you would experience abundant life! How could it be any other way? Jesus is *the* Good Shepherd, *your* Good Shepherd. The transforming power of the gospel not only changes our eternal destiny, it also impacts every day of our lives here on earth.

85

Take a moment to review your list of desires. I encourage you to repent of any wrong desires *and* anything you have made more important than pleasing God. Repentance means to turn in a new direction. When you turn to Jesus for forgiveness, his Holy Spirit will help you turn from your self-centered desires and turn toward Christ, who will change you to be like him (1 John 1:9). The Lord has made you his own and, according to Romans 8:31–39, he has freely given you all things. There is nothing you lack. Surrender your heart to him. As you do, Jesus can change your desires so that your words reflect a love for God and others.

Jesus Wants to Change Your Communication

How does Jesus change our desires? It happens as we turn away from self-centered desires and reflect on all Christ has done and is doing. As we grow in our love for him and our desires focus on pleasing him, the way we communicate will change. Our hearts are the source of all we do and say, so when our hearts love Jesus, loving actions follow. God calls all who are saved to live out his Word in practical ways. Ephesians 2:8–9 talks about our salvation, and verse 10 then describes a loving response to our salvation: "For we are his workmanship, created in Christ Jesus for good works, which God prepared beforehand, that we should walk in them." For those who love Jesus, this is not drudgery (although it can be a struggle); instead, it is a privilege and a joy.

You might be thinking, "I am growing in my love for Jesus and I know my communication flows from my heart, but does the Bible give any practical tools to improve my communication?" The answer is an overwhelming YES. In our counseling ministry, thousands have been helped by the practical communication principles outlined in the Bible.[3] The four principles below pro-vide specific direction on how to live out your love for Jesus in the way you speak.

Four Communication Principles

The Bible has a lot to say about communication, and this book cannot summarize it all. However, one of the best texts on communication is Ephesians 4:25–32. To understand this passage, let's consider the context. In Ephesians 4:17–24, Paul explains that when you trust Christ as your Lord and Savior, there is a radical change in your thoughts and behavior. You are a new person in Christ, in union with him. You have the Holy Spirit within you, so you can live as an ambassador for Jesus. God changes your heart so that you can live a changed life. Paul explains that a believer should not act like an unbeliever but should exchange sinful patterns for godly ones. This process of becoming like Christ (progressive sanctification) takes place as our minds are renewed (see also Romans 12:1–2) by the grace of God.

When you put James 4:1–2 and Ephesians 4:17–24 together, you see that anything we put in the center of our life in place of Christ needs to be put off—rejected. A new way of thinking and behaving must be embraced. In Ephesians 4, Paul explains several aspects of this new way of thinking and behaving; most have some relationship to communication.

Truth 1: Be honest

> Therefore, having put away falsehood, let each one
> of you speak the truth with his neighbor, for we are
> members one of another. (Ephesians 4:25)

---

3. Jay Adams may have been the first to list these truths this way. At Faith, we have used them for years because they are so practical and memorable.

At first glance, honesty seems so simple. Yet all too often our communication contains various forms of deceit. For example, (1) lying, no matter how small or "innocent" the lie might be; (2) body language and words that do not seem to match; (3) exaggerating without letting our audience know we are exaggerating; or (4) using absolute words like *never* or *always*. In the fourth example, our communication does not accurately represent the facts. Instead, our words tell others how good we are or how lousy they are. The truth is that your boss is not *always* mean, your spouse is not *always* insensitive, and your coworker is not *always* rude. While honesty is not easy, especially in a conversation that is emotionally charged, verse 25 explains that we need to be honest because "we are members of one another." You cannot build meaningful relationships unless you are willing to be honest even when it is hard. The Bible says that wounds from a friend are faithful (even though they are still wounds) and they are much better than the kisses from an enemy (Proverbs 27:6). In marriage, we need to learn to receive such words from our spouse.

If you focus more on your love for Jesus and find joy in your relationship with him, you will begin to communicate honestly. You can work hard to express the real issue instead of hiding behind a false one. As a result, each of you can trust what the other is saying and you can talk about the real issues in your lives. All marriages have struggles and challenges, but honesty is not only the best policy, it is Christ-centered policy. Your honest communication, expressed wisely, will build your relationship and give you many years of joy together.

Truth 2: Solve problems quickly

> Be angry and do not sin; do not let the sun go down
> on your anger, and give no opportunity to the devil.
> (Ephesians 4:26–27)

Couples often struggle to solve today's problems today. They either go unresolved or the attempts to resolve them only end up creating more problems. Unresolved problems can lead to bitterness (Hebrews 12:15). Bitterness is evident when a problem is brought up again and again to criticize and condemn. Over time, the bitterness associated with unresolved problems grows so large that no meaningful relationship is possible until the bitterness is removed. Instead of solving today's problems today, individuals are forced to deal with a lot of past baggage.

As you put this rule into practice, you will discover that keeping the relationship clear of problems is not as hard as you thought. Imagine if you never, ever said to each other, "Remember fourteen years ago when . . ." or brought up old issues to add to new ones. If Jesus is at the center of your communication commitment, you will rarely live with unresolved conflict for more than a day.

Now that I have been married for over twenty years, I greatly enjoy the comforts of home. It is a place of refuge because conflict, when it occurs, is put down quickly. This is not impossible, even for two sinners like us who are saved by grace. It can happen if Jesus is kept at the center of your life and you rely on his strength to love as he loved you.

Truth 3: Be encouraging instead of attacking

> Let no corrupting talk come out of your mouths, but
> only such as is good for building up, as fits the occasion,
> that it may give grace to those who hear. (Ephesians 4:29)

This principle applies when two people are trying to deal with a problem: one person attacks the other instead of dealing with the issue at hand. Not focusing on the problem can lead to personal attacks that hurt the relationship and create a new set of problems. Ephesians 4:29 tells us that this is opposite to what God intends. Our words should be conduits for grace, not weapons for conflict.

But notice that Ephesians 4:29 was not written simply for problem solving. Imagine that the vast majority of the communication you had with your fiancé(e) was characterized by "building up" or "edifying" speech. Imagine that you spent so much time telling each other about the good things that you only had a little time to talk about problems. That would be a relationship characterized by joy.

I truly believe it can be this way if you choose to worship Jesus through the use of encouraging words. Sending thoughtful and caring text messages, thanking each other for the ways your future spouse is a blessing to you, and speaking about each other in kind ways will do much to please Jesus and build your marriage.

Truth 4: Act, don't react

> Let all bitterness and wrath and anger and clamor and
> slander be put away from you, along with all malice. Be
> kind to one another, tenderhearted, forgiving one another,
> as God in Christ forgave you. (Ephesians 4:31–32)

There is much to discuss in verses 31–32, but two points in particular stand out. First, there are certain responses (actions) that should always be part of the way we communicate—words that express gentleness, forgiveness, and kindness. Would those who work with you describe your communication that way?

Second, certain kinds of communication (reactions) are sinful and need to be stopped—words that express malice, clamor, and slander. Why? Because these things do not please the Lord. Are you quick to point out others' faults? Do you use a harsh tone? Do you assume the worst of people and then share your worst thoughts with others, so that they will think the worst about people as well?

I know that I live out these four communication patterns very imperfectly. Maybe you realize that about yourself too. But the end of verse 32 provides something wonderful for us—a way to deal with the times we dishonor the Lord with our speech. Whenever you fail, ask God to forgive you. Then, having received the amazing forgiveness of Jesus, you can forgive each other.

Relationship Building for Life

Godly communication has value for a lifetime. It will take time, effort, faith, humility, and energy to change your desires and actions to reflect Jesus at the center of your life, but the results are well worth it! You can have a marriage as God intended it, full of joy, love, compassion, and blessing. Your ability to strengthen relationships in the home, in the workplace, or in your local church will increase as you turn to Christ for the help you need to live for him instead of for yourself. Paul tells us in 2 Corinthians that when we are controlled by the love of Christ, we no longer live for ourselves, but for Jesus.

> For the love of Christ controls us, because we have concluded this: that one has died for all, therefore all have died; and he died for all, that those who live might no longer live for themselves but for him who for their sake died and was raised. (2 Corinthians 5:14–15)

When you make your aim to please Christ, his Spirit will help you build others up with your communication. As you do that, your relationships will become characterized by honesty, kindness, grace, and forgiveness.

Homework Discussion Questions

Complete the following questions on your own and then share your answers with your fiancé(e). Later, discuss your answers and your conversation as a couple with your mentor.

Think deeply about these questions. Shallow answers will hurt you and your future spouse more than anyone else. Deeper, more honest answers may lead to some uncomfortable moments, but that is okay. These real-life discussions will help you to prepare and learn as a couple.

1. Compare how each of you answered the two questions earlier in this chapter.
   a. Do you think your fiancé(e) has correctly identified the desires that motivate him or her?
   b. Do you have any suggestions for your fiancé(e) to consider about either answer?
2. Make a bullet list of how you tend to communicate with people you see often (coworkers, parents, or friends). What biblical principles do you apply? Which do you neglect or violate?
3. Write down three areas in your relationship that could be challenging in the days ahead. What concerns you about those particular areas? (For example, if a bride is bringing a son into the marriage who still has a relationship with his biological father, both the wife and new husband may be concerned about their communication about parenting.)
4. Be ready to explain where communication comes from and how it is changed. What are the four rules of communication listed in this chapter?
5. What two statements in this chapter had the most impact on you? What particularly struck you about them? Be prepared to discuss this with each other and with your mentor.
6. Choose the most significant Bible passage in this chapter. Write it on an index card and review it daily until your appointment with your mentor.
7. What truths have you learned about Christ that can help you to reject ungodly desires and choose to please Christ in your speech? For example, what have you learned about his

love, his suffering for you, his role as an intercessor, or his promise to never abandon you?

8. Why do you think you need the grace that comes from Christ to help you communicate according to these principles?

9. If you have seen ways that your communication is not all God wants it to be, list the ways you need to repent—and do it!

10. Spend at least five minutes daily praying for you and your future spouse, that Jesus would truly be the center of your life and that your communication with each other would be biblical.

Advanced Homework

Couples may find this additional homework option encouraging and beneficial.

- Read *War of Words* by Paul Tripp (Phillipsburg, NJ: P&R Publishing, 2000). This book describes two kingdoms and two types of communication. You may find the kingdom analogy particularly helpful.

Chapter 6

Finances with Jesus as the Center

AS YOU MAKE your way through this curriculum, I hope it is helping you see that the more you love Jesus and find practical ways to honor him in your relationship with your future spouse, the more you will enjoy the benefits God intended for marriage. This is certainly true when it comes to money. Some say that money is the issue that couples argue about most, but it does not have to be that way. It is possible to find joy in using money as a means to honor and worship Jesus. This chapter will discuss some heart issues related to money and offer some tools for money management, but let me begin with a few practical comments.

Take Inventory

Before you continue reading, please gather the following documents:

- A current budget for you as an individual
- A first-draft budget for your first year of marriage
- A list of all your assets and debts (i.e., a net worth statement)
- Last year's state and federal tax returns. If you have been out of school for more than three years, bring your returns from two years ago as well.

This information can help your mentor understand your past financial decisions as well as your plans for spending money in the future. Please read this chapter slowly. Think about each point and compare each point to the actual numbers on your documents.

Key Truths to Remember

Managing money is not simply about making a budget in which your income is higher than your expenses. Christ-centered money management is about using the resources God has loaned you to have the most impact for the cause of Christ.

People argue about money because they have their own ideas on how it should be spent. However, the more you both worship Jesus, love him, want to serve him, and desire to make him the center of your life, the more you will both seek to honor the Lord financially, and the more agreement you will find in this area.

With your documents and this overarching principle in mind, consider how the following five truths can help you honor the Lord with your money.

Truth # 1: You are not an owner, you are a steward

Stewardship refers to much more than finances (as the passages below demonstrate), but it certainly includes finances. The sooner you remember that God owns everything, the sooner you will be able to worship the Lord with your money and the less you will have an entitlement mentality.

> As each has received a gift, use it to serve one another, as good stewards of God's varied grace: whoever speaks, as one who speaks oracles of God; whoever serves, as one who serves by the strength that God supplies—in order that in everything God may be glorified through Jesus

Christ. To him belong glory and dominion forever and ever. Amen. (1 Peter 4:10–11)

This is how one should regard us, as servants of Christ and stewards of the mysteries of God. Moreover, it is required of stewards that they be found faithful. (1 Corinthians 4:1–2)

As a steward of all that God has given you, it is your responsibility and joy to consider how Jesus, your Master, would want you to use those resources. God entrusts you with everything you have: your intellect, your abilities, your skills, and the money those things produce. They are not meant to be used in a self-centered way, but in a way that points you and others to the glory of Christ. You may have been given the opportunity to steward large amounts of money, while others have the privilege to steward less. The issue is not how much you have, but what you do with what you have.

Christian financial writer Ron Blue says, "Every spending decision is a spiritual decision." He is right, because every spending decision reflects what you think of the Lord Jesus. I once worked with a couple who had accumulated a lot of debt. As I was teaching this truth, the man stopped me and asked, "Are you saying that God cares about whether I buy a sixty-cent can of pop on my break?" "Absolutely," I said, "because when you start thinking about the Lord as you stand in front of the vending machine, you will also think about him at the car lot, when you are planning a vacation, and when you are ready to buy the next great electronic gadget that will supposedly make your life much easier."

Truth # 2: You must guard your heart against greed

The Lord has given us a lot. In fact, it would take far too long to list all the gifts the Bible says the Lord has given. But here are five of those gifts:

- He has given us every spiritual blessing in the heavenly places (Ephesians 1:3)
- He has given us the forgiveness of our sins (Ephesians 1:7)
- We have an eternal inheritance reserved in heaven for us (Ephesians 1:11)
- We have the presence of God, the indwelling Holy Spirit, every moment of our lives (Ephesians 1:14)
- Since God did not spare his own Son, he will freely give us all things (Romans 8:32)

We have truly been given a lot—everything we need, in fact. But when greed penetrates our hearts, it communicates messages like:

- You have nothing
- You will be happy if you have _____
- You deserve more
- You have a right to _____

This leads engaged or newly married couples to seek to acquire in two years what it took their parents thirty years to accumulate. I have watched young married couples buy new cars and homes right on the edge of their budget. They accumulate debt on all sorts of purchases from vacations to furniture to unexpected expenses. After several years, they are faced with very difficult choices that make it easy to argue with each other and make it hard to worship Jesus.

But if you guard your heart against greed right now, you won't have to live with the consequences of greedy choices. A powerful Bible passage on the subject of greed is Luke 12:13–21. Jesus was teaching a large crowd, warning them against the Pharisees. He explained that suffering may come to those who follow Christ but that the suffering would be worth it. In the middle of this, a man stands up and asks Jesus to arbitrate a family financial dispute.

Apparently this man believed he was entitled to a larger inheritance than he had received (v. 13). This man's question had nothing to do with what Jesus was talking about. Apparently the man did not care about Jesus's teaching; he just wanted Jesus to come to his defense.

Jesus's response is a soft rebuke. He refuses to judge this man's dispute with his family, but expresses concern with his attitude. He warns the entire crowd in verse 15 to beware and be on their guard against all forms of greed. In an ironic twist, Jesus uses this man's question to teach everyone about the dangers of greed.

Jesus follows with a simple story to teach about greed (vv. 16–21). A rich man had very productive fields. Instead of being a good and generous steward of God's blessings, he chose to be greedy. He believed that there were certain things he deserved. Thus, his plan (vv. 17–19) is filled with references to himself (count the number of "I"s and "me"s in those three verses).

We can make a couple of practical applications from this text.

Application 1: Make every effort to avoid the seduction of greed

Look at your current budget, your first draft budget for your first year of marriage, and your debt load. Then ask yourself if greed is or has been present. Are you committing too much to housing because you want a certain kind of home right away? Are you committing too much to vehicles because you like the smell of a new car? What about entertainment?

I am not proposing that you live on a dirt floor, drive a junker, and never buy anything but Ramen Noodles. (That would create different stewardship issues!) I am asking you to evaluate your financial documents from the perspective of greed. Search your heart deeply because greed is very seductive. This is an exercise you should repeat every year. As your financial condition changes, greed will look for every opportunity to gain a foothold.

Application 2: Remember that riches are not the sum total of life

A "life" does not consist of what one owns. A person's identity must be found in Christ, not in the way he looks, the way he dresses, the house he owns, or the size of his bank account. The world may be impressed with nice things, but Jesus looks at the heart. He is not as concerned about the quality of our clothes as he is concerned about the quality of our character.

I can empathize with anyone who has given in to greed. One personal story will suffice, although there are many others. A couple of years ago, some of my friends encouraged me to register for a triathlon. I once rode a ten-speed, but that was before the last Ice Age, so all I had was a cheap imitation mountain bike that I bought at Walmart. As soon as I started riding with my friends on road bikes, I suddenly understood the difference. I was working as hard as I could and they were barely peddling. I *needed* a road bike. The more I rode the mountain bike, the more I could hear my greed calling out to me, "You would be happy if you had that $3,000 carbon fiber bike." There was no doubt that a road bike would make training with my friends a lot easier, but would it make me happy? Here was a moment where Jesus had to be at the center of my life. Jesus is the only one who can give me joy and satisfaction. I needed to think rightly about the bike, not simply from a stewardship perspective, but also from the perspective of what would make me happy. A bike would make training easier and longer events more realistic, but I could not buy a bike until I had properly thought about issues of stewardship and greed.

Greed is often at the forefront of debt. It is an attitude of the heart that is unwilling to wait or to do without, so debt is often a part of the equation. Money and possessions cannot buy happiness. That is why you must be so diligent to avoid greed. The following questions may help you evaluate your susceptibility to greed:

1. Do you purchase items that you don't have the money to buy?
2. Do you believe that having _____
   (i.e., a particular item) will make you happy? What does that say about your view of your riches in Christ?
3. Do you use bonuses for vacations and luxuries when you have consumer debt that remains unpaid?
4. How do you draw the distinction between being greedy and not being greedy?

So far we have covered two truths about finances—stewardship and greed. Now consider your budget, your debts, and your assets. What observations can you make?

Truth 3: Contentment is critical because it communicates that you value God's presence

> Keep your life free from love of money, and be content with what you have, for he has said, "I will never leave you nor forsake you." So we can confidently say, "The Lord is my helper; I will not fear; what can man do to me?" (Hebrews 13:5–6)

The writer of Hebrews makes a connection between God's presence and our ability to deal with challenges. In essence, God's presence is enough. The fact that Hebrews includes this passage is even more significant because Hebrews was written to people who had lost their homes (10:32) and suffered in many ways, including financially. Yet the overarching reason to be content given in the passage is the ongoing presence of God.

When a person recognizes and appreciates the presence of God, she understands that everything she needs comes from Christ (Romans 8:32). Once we are content and free from the love of money, we no longer have to pursue it or live for it.

The book of Philippians also includes a very important passage on contentment: Philippians 4:13, "I can do all things through him who strengthens me." We see in the passage that *Contentment is a state of Christ-empowered gladness or joy in the midst of God-ordained circumstances that cannot be changed at the time.*

Paul had probably been imprisoned for four years before writing Philippians. While this imprisonment was not akin to the horror stories we sometimes hear about, it was nevertheless a restricted and unpleasant environment. Yet Paul does not spend his time complaining. Instead, he rejoices that by God's grace he has learned to be content with what he has, whether it is a lot or a little. He later wrote to Timothy, one of the people he loved and mentored, "If we have food and covering, with these we will be content" (1 Timothy 6:8).

Paul's contentment, however, was not possible in his own strength. As we see in this passage, Paul confesses that the source of his contentment is Christ.

The issue of contentment based on God's presence has huge implications for the way people spend money. Many people ask the question, "Can I afford it?" But the deeper and more biblical question is, "Would the Lord be pleased by this?"

Even if I have enough money to go to Starbucks on a daily basis, would I be a good steward to use God's money that way? The question is not rhetorical. Some people benefit by using their money this way. I believe Scripture is clear that we can and should use some of what God has given us to celebrate his goodness and kindness to us (Deuteronomy 14:22–27). Thus, some people may celebrate the Lord's blessings through a regular visit to Starbucks while others celebrate God's goodness through other choices. At the same time, this may be a sinful indulgence for some. The same question could be asked about dinners out or entertainment choices like cable or satellite dish. In fact, the contentment question pertains to almost every spending decision you will ever make.

To create a financial plan that deals with significant heart issues like stewardship, greed, and contentment, Christ has to be at the center of your life.

Truth 4: You must exercise wisdom to become biblical planners

> Go to the ant, O sluggard; consider her ways, and be wise. Without having any chief, officer, or ruler, she prepares her bread in summer and gathers her food in harvest. (Proverbs 6:6–8)

In this passage, a father is instructing his son, preparing him for life. One of the life lessons he delivered was the importance of being a wise planner. As you read this text, one question seems to jump off the page: If the ant had used up all his resources in the summer, then, when winter came, could the ant say that the Lord did not provide for him?

Some married couples have done just that. The Lord provides them with a certain income and they use all of it for the things they want. Then, when an emergency arises, they cry out to the Lord wanting more. The Lord is so gracious and kind that he sometimes fulfills that need immediately. But at other times, he permits a measure of suffering to help his children learn from their foolishness.

It is true, of course, that future planning should always be done "if the Lord wills" (James 4:15). Planning always reveals the value we place on our personal relationship with Christ. When Jesus is at the center, wise plans are made and there is a willingness to say "no" in the present to prepare for something in the future. Yet the attitude in planning is "as the Lord wills."

The impact of biblical planning on the family budget is profound. Imagine a couple that did not plan for oil changes, new tires, home repairs, car or life insurance, or medical expenses. Items like these should have a place in the family budget. What about clothing?

It would be nice, I suppose, if our clothes lasted forty years like those God preserved during the wilderness wanderings. But most of the time, things need to be replaced much sooner.

The same can be said for vacations. It may be that a family can only plan an expensive vacation every few years, while taking much less expensive trips the other years. This is exactly where contentment is needed. Your friends or family members may be free to do things that you simply cannot or should not do. Yet Christ can strengthen and encourage you in moments like these.

Once these items are included in your budget, they may impact the resources that are available for larger purchases like a car or a home. While it may not be feasible right away, I encourage you to plan to purchase your vehicles with cash. Most likely this will require you to be content with an older model.

Think carefully about priorities. There are regular monthly expenses, short-term planning expenses (like repairs, insurance, etc.) and longer term needs like retirement and college tuition. Young couples starting out probably won't be able to address all these concerns at once, but the wise, godly planner will have one eye on the present and one eye on potential issues coming in the future.

Truth 5: Be generous and sacrificial in your giving

Remember, everything belongs to the Lord. Theologically, there is no such thing as "your money." Instead, you are stewarding God's resources for his honor and glory. Part of that stewardship is giving, especially to your local church. Regular and sacrificial giving is the means God uses to provide for the needs associated with ministry. Giving is also an opportunity to tangibly express thanks for all that the Lord has done for you.

One of the most important New Testament passages on giving is 2 Corinthians 8–9. Please take a few minutes to read the text. It makes two important points about generosity.

Generosity is to be sacrificial. Perhaps the clearest emphasis is on generosity as sacrifice. In Luke 21, Jesus talked about this when he stood in the temple and contrasted the well-to-do Pharisees, whose large contributions had little impact on their spiritual life, and the poor widow, whose contribution was meaningless to the treasury budget and yet significant in the sight of God. Her sacrificial giving demonstrated her love for God and her faith and reliance on him.

In Corinth, a collection was being taken for struggling believers in Judea. Corinth was a large and wealthy city, and it appears that Paul hoped, perhaps even expected, the Corinthians to give sizeable amounts since they were able to do so. However, Paul mentions another group, the Macedonians, who were more rural and much poorer, with material needs of their own. Yet their willingness to participate in this collection demonstrated their concern both for God and for their brothers and sisters in Christ. They were an example for the Corinthians to follow.

The Macedonians recognized the value of following the Lord in the matter of generous giving. They knew that this would require a sacrifice on their part, but it would relieve some of the burden on their fellow Christians.

Generosity is a privilege. In 2 Corinthians 8, several phrases about the Macedonians indicate that they saw giving as a privilege, including "abundance of joy" (v. 2), "begging us earnestly" (v. 4), "they gave . . . beyond their means, of their own accord" (v. 3), and "gave themselves first to the Lord" (v. 5).

Their desire was to help. They wanted to participate in supporting the saints (vv. 3–5). They willingly and happily made personal sacrifices to do so, even begging to be included because they saw generosity as part of their stewardship before the Lord.

The text says that they "gave themselves first to the Lord." This implies that they recognized where their funds had come from. They recognized who provided for them. The question is whether or not we see giving as a privilege. Is it something we rejoice over? When we get to the end of the year, can we look at our giving records and rejoice that God gave us the opportunity to do something productive with our money? When we give to others, are we thankful that God has put us in the position to be generous?

We have looked at several truths about our hearts and our finances, demonstrating again that Jesus must be the center of our lives and the gospel needs to influence every area of life.

1. The gospel of Jesus says that I and all I have belong to God; therefore I must be a good steward of it.
2. The gospel of Jesus promises that I own all things already in Christ, so I don't need to be greedy.
3. The gospel of Jesus assures me that his presence (Hebrews 13:5–6) can help me to be content.
4. The gospel of Jesus demonstrates God's glorious wisdom, a wisdom I should emulate in my planning.
5. The gospel of Jesus reminds me that it is a privilege to give to the Lord.

Knowing all that helps us when, at some point, we must put numbers on a page and make a budget. But the numbers must be biblically informed numbers. What does that mean? A lot of practical financial advice suggests certain percentages of one's income for various expenses, but the Bible does not list percentages. There is flexibility regarding the way people choose to organize their finances. What God cares about is the way the beliefs, desires, and commitments of our hearts direct our use of money. Is Jesus at the center of all those things?

Creating a Budget

To create a budget for your first year of married life, begin with your income. You may have stable employment that will continue into your marriage or you may be just starting out in the working world. Either way, think through your situation to determine what you believe would be a conservative estimate of your income. (It's always easier to increase a budget than to decrease it.)

You will also need to decide if you will budget based on one income or two. While children may be down the road for many couples, it is important not to create a budget that unnecessarily limits your options for the future. For example, if a future bride hopes to be a stay-at-home mom eventually, it is important not to use her income for normal monthly expenses. Instead, you could use her income to pay for a particular project or to build your savings.

Once you determine your income, you should prioritize your expenses based on the biblical principles discussed earlier. Things like giving should be high priorities, along with groceries and transportation. Insurance should be a high priority as well as some emergency and repair expenses. Once you cover these basics, you are free to determine the rest based on your desires and your available income. Some couples will place a high value on where they live, but that may be offset by inexpensive cars and vacations. Others will enjoy eating out regularly but will sacrifice where they live in order to do so. In the end, however, all your income should be accounted for either in an expense or savings category.

When you have completed your budget, go back through this chapter and see if your budget reflects biblical principles on financial management.

A System of Management

In addition to a budget, you need a management system. Once again, there is no "Thus says the Lord" for how a couple chooses to manage their finances. The blessing of a good system is that it helps you to manage your finances in a way that reflects your heart for Christ. There are several keys to making a system work.

1. Use a system you understand. Some people create really complicated systems that look impressive but are open to user error. You want a simple system that works for you.
2. Use a system that allows you as a couple to function without conflict. If my wife and I had a conflict over money, it was almost always about receipts. We had a budget, so we did not argue about what we spent, only that we needed to keep receipts to track actual expenses. We realized that we needed a system that allowed for some "losing of receipts" while also giving us excellent controls of our spending.
3. Choose a system you will use. A system is only good if you actually use it!

Our system (which is certainly not the only way or even the right way) may give you a few ideas. I do all our tracking in a spreadsheet. One sheet is dedicated to the budget. It lists income and expenses. A second sheet is dedicated to tracking the way we implement the budget. This second sheet has expenses broken into five categories.

- Short-term savings placed in a money market account. These are savings for things like a car or home repair. There is no regularity to these expenses. I can't predict, for example, when my dishwasher will break or my car will need to be fixed. But I have saved for these expenses whenever they happen.

- Short-term savings placed in our checking account. This covers items like trash collection or car insurance. These bills are very regular (quarterly, semi-annually, or annually). I place money for them in the checking account to ensure that I have the money when they are due. It keeps me from running my checking balance into the danger zone.
- Monthly bills. We have ten bills per month, every month. The money for them is in the checking account so they can be paid. These include expenses like our mortgage.
- Expenses paid with cash. Each month we use an envelope system for things like fuel, family money, and groceries. Let's say we withdraw $400 per month to feed our family of five. To track expenses we assume that all $400 is spent, even if there is a little money left in the envelope. This means that cash expenses to do not require receipts.
- Miscellaneous expenses. This is the most complicated part of our system. We use two check registries with our checking account. Each month, a certain amount is given to the second checkbook to handle any expenses that fit into the miscellaneous category. Again, there is no need for receipts, just updating the registry when money is spent.

This system works beautifully for us. A simple spreadsheet and process have made management a pretty easy task, usually taking about two hours per month.

This system is a modified version of the system found in Ron Blue's *Managing Your Money*, but you can use any system that works. However, it is important to speak with your mentor about the heart issues involved in finances and how they will play out in your circumstances.

If you do this, you will be in a position to enjoy what God has given you as a steward of his grace. You will also find that there can be wonderful unity as a couple in the area of finances. If the old saying is correct that ninety percent of all marital conflicts occur over money, sex, and children, then this chapter will help you decrease your conflicts by a third! Having a plan for your finances not only honors the Lord, it will be an incredible blessing to you and your family.

Homework Discussion Questions

Complete the following questions on your own and then share your answers with your fiancé(e). Later, discuss your answers and your conversation as a couple with your mentor.

1. What priorities do you have when it comes to finances? (Saving vs. spending, giving vs. no giving, housing vs. cars, debt for something you want vs. waiting until you have the financial resources).
2. Before you read this chapter, what biblical principles about money did you know? What truths have you learned by reading this chapter?
3. Explain in your own words why "every spending decision is a spiritual decision."
4. In what area of financial management do you believe you are weakest?
5. What two statements impacted you most in this chapter? What struck you about them? Be prepared to discuss this with each other and with your mentor.
6. Skim this chapter again and choose the Bible passage most significant to you. Write it on an index card and review it each day until your appointment with your mentor.
7. What truths have you learned about Christ that would give you a heart that allows Jesus to influence your use of money?
8. Why do you think it is important to rely on the grace provided by Jesus in order to manage money biblically?

9. If you believe that your financial stewardship has not been entirely pleasing to God, list the ways you need to repent— and do it!

10. Spend at least five minutes daily praying for yourself and your future spouse, that Jesus would truly be the center of your life together and that your finances would honor Christ.

Advanced Homework

Here is an additional homework possibility that couples may find helpful.

- Read *Neither Poverty Nor Riches* by Craig Blomberg (Downers Grove, IL: InterVarsity Press, 1999). This book traces a biblical theology of money through the Old and New Testaments. It shows that having a lot and having a little are both potentially dangerous spiritually.

Chapter 7

Community with Jesus as the Center

AS FAR AS I know, premarital resources rarely, if ever, discuss the importance of the local church. But as I study Scripture and watch young couples establish patterns for their marriage, I have come to believe that a chapter like this belongs in a book like this. Community is an important issue to discuss because God designed us to be in community. The community God desires for his people has several different components. As you prepare to build a life together, community will play a significant part in your happiness and ongoing growth.

My wife and I learned how important community was when we began our marriage. At first we lived just minutes away from both sets of parents. Our parents were not nosy or interfering in our relationship. They allowed us to initiate most of our contact. As a result, neither my wife nor I felt threatened or pressured in our relationships with our parents. It was normal for us to spend time with them twice a month and occasionally more often. I learned to snow ski because my dad and I joined the ski club at my father's place of employment. For eight weeks we drove to the local ski resort for lessons and practice time. Not only did we learn to ski, our relationship as adults grew. In our relationship with our parents, Stephanie and I were not dependent on them, but we were only ten minutes from love, care, concern, and help. We felt very secure.

At the same time, my wife and I were heavily invested in our local church. We had been there a number of years before our marriage and our connections remained after the wedding. We served in the youth group with leaders who mentored us and gave us opportunities to serve. In those early days, my wife and I also had jobs where we achieved success. Both of us enjoyed the blessing of recognition and the fruit that came with it. So we had a work community that was partially responsible for making fifty hours each week fairly enjoyable.

In short, Stephanie and I had a lot of community when we got married. Our lives were full of it! But we did not realize what we had until the Lord led us to move from our hometown to another part of the country for seminary training. The day we moved, Stephanie was seven months pregnant with our first child. I registered for a full load of classes and I had a thirty-two-hour-a-week job to pay the bills. Stephanie did not work outside the home.

In one week we lost the family community we had known our whole lives, we lost our work communities where we had been successful, we lost the church community that had been significant to us, and we lost the comfort of our hometown, which always just "felt" like home. Within three months we were drowning in self-pity. We had a new church, we were the parents of a newborn, we were in the midst of seminary training, and we had people who cared about us. But our focus was on all we had lost. It was easy to complain about missing family, about when stores were closed, about how far it was to certain restaurants, and about the quality of the church. Without realizing it, we were on the path to destroying ourselves.

By God's grace and the Spirit's work in our lives, we learned to repent of our sour attitudes. But looking back, I realize I failed as a leader by not ensuring that there was Christian community for Stephanie and me. Sadly, the Lord had to teach us by experience what we had often read in his Word: we were designed for community. We wish we'd listened to his Word and avoided the consequences of our choices.

You may choose to live near family or you may be separated from them by significant distance. You may have a wonderful community at work or it may be a challenge to become part of the team. Both family and work communities are valuable, but they are not essential for spiritual health. But there is one kind of community that you cannot live without, namely, the body of Christ.

Community in the Body of Christ

The body of Christ is the universal church—that is, all believers in Christ (1 Corinthians 12:12–27). Yet most every New Testament letter is written to an individual church or a group of churches located in the same city, including the letter of 1 Corinthians— that is, to local churches. Believers in Christ were expected to be involved in their local body or they were expected to start one. There were no other options. As a future husband, this is an opportunity for you to be a meaningful spiritual leader.

Finding a church home, if you do not already have one, can be a challenge. You may have deep wounds from the sinful behavior of people in a church you once belonged to—it may have even involved a church leader. This makes you reluctant to consider joining another church. I certainly can understand that concern, but I think it is also important to understand that you are starting a new life with your spouse. You need community, not just for yourself as an individual, but for your marriage. So, prayerfully, commit yourself to finding a church home. Jesus promised to build his church and he wants it to be a place where you and your spouse both give and receive. Here are three tips to make the process easier.

First, attend a church three to four weeks in a row. It is difficult to understand a church until you have been there multiple times. It is especially important to visit several weeks in a row if one of your visits occurs on a special day like Mother's Day. Holidays often are not a true picture of that church's weekly ministry.

Second, visit whatever ministry the church uses to connect people to each other. The Sunday worship service is often the worst place in a church to get connected. Everyone faces a platform where all the action occurs and the worship service is the most crowded event in the church. Take time to visit a small group or a Sunday school class. In my church, we have observed that people are far more likely to leave the church within two years if they are not connected to our small groups. If you don't visit the ministries designed to connect people, you won't learn how the church does community.

Third, attend the church's membership class. They are often led by the senior pastor, or at least the senior staff. This is a great opportunity to get to know the church, what they believe, and how new people can get connected. Obviously, this process requires a bit of time, but few people have to do this two or three times before they find a church home. Even if you have family nearby and your job is one you have had for a while, you are still in need of local church community.

Part of making Jesus the center of your life and your marriage will involve finding, joining, and being involved in a local church community. To maximize its benefit to you and your spouse, aim at faithfully attending, joining, and serving in a church within three months of your wedding. Let's consider three primary purposes for church community.

To Encourage You to Love and Serve

Let us hold fast the confession of our hope without wavering, for he who promised is faithful. And let us consider how to stir up one another to love and good

works, not neglecting to meet together, as is the habit of
some, but encouraging one another, and all the more as
you see the Day drawing near. (Hebrews 10:23–25)

The book of Hebrews was written for a group of suffering
Christians living in a challenging world. Their society was against
them in almost every way. Some had suffered persecution and all of
them experienced living in a culture that thought differently than
they did. That sounds a lot like today, doesn't it? We live in a world
whose values are often at odds with the truth of God's Word. Who
is going to encourage us to live according to truth? It will not be
the media, the entertainment industry, the school system, or most
office environments. The encouragement to live godly lives will
come primarily from the church.

I have seen the pain of many destructive marriages. It aches to
even write about them. In almost every case, the couples were iso-
lated rather than living in community with Christians who loved
them, cared for them, and encouraged them to love others. That
does not mean that they did not attend church, for many did. But
outside of the Sunday morning service, they had virtually no meaningful Christian contact the rest of the week.

Living in community also encourages our service, the good
works Hebrews talks about. It is so easy to think only about what
I want. This focus on self feeds our inner "Me-Monster." The more
we feed it, the worse it becomes. But the church is where we are
encouraged to do good deeds with gratitude for all we have received
from God, and with a vision for how God can use us to further his
purposes on earth. The church encourages us to look beyond ourselves to the needs of others (Galatians 6:9–10).

Again, it is easy to see why Jesus must be at the center of our lives
as individuals and as a couple. Jesus promised to build his church
and the gates of hell would not be able to overcome it (Matthew
16:18). If the church is important to Jesus and Jesus is the center of

our lives, the church will be important to us. One of your first tasks, if you have not done so already, is to find a church home where the encouragement to serve occurs regularly.

To Equip You to Mature in the Christian Faith

> And he gave the apostles, the prophets, the evangelists, the shepherds and teachers, to equip the saints for the work of ministry, for building up the body of Christ, until we all attain to the unity of the faith and of the knowledge of the Son of God, to mature manhood, to the measure of the stature of the fullness of Christ, so that we may no longer be children, tossed to and fro by the waves and carried about by every wind of doctrine, by human cunning, by craftiness in deceitful schemes. Rather, speaking the truth in love, we are to grow up in every way into him who is the head, into Christ, from whom the whole body, joined and held together by every joint with which it is equipped, when each part is working properly, makes the body grow so that it builds itself up in love. (Ephesians 4:11–16)

The first reason emphasized the role of the church in helping us do something productive with our lives. Where we might be tempted to just focus on ourselves, we will be encouraged to love and serve others. But that implies that we know *how* to love and serve others. Thus, we see a second key role for the church. The second reason that the church is vital to your life and marriage is that the church is the place where your Christian faith can grow. In Ephesians 4, Christ specifically gifts his church with certain individuals (apostles, prophets, evangelists, shepherds, and teachers). These individuals have a clear job description: to equip the saints for the work of ministry. That doesn't mean that they do no ministry themselves. It simply means that they are expected to equip and train other people—namely, you.

This equipping and training involves several things. It includes teaching the Word. Many Christians open their Bibles and struggle to understand it. The poetic literature can be intimidating, the argument of an epistle can be complicated, and some texts are just plain hard to sort out. A pastor is to teach what the Bible says and how to understand it for oneself. So it is important to look for a church where the Scriptures are taught clearly. But that is not all there is to equipping.

Pastors/shepherds are also called to exercise leadership and authority that results in people becoming more faithful followers of Jesus. While the analogy is not exact, I think a pastor is much like a coach. The coach decides what skills, strength, conditioning, and learning are most needed to help his players improve. Sometimes this requires strenuous workouts and repetition, sometimes study or rest. Players are responsible to follow the coach's leadership in order to improve. Pastors are called to think, pray, teach, and lead their people to take the steps most necessary for their growth and maturity. Therefore, it is important to find a church where you will be led and motivated to grow. Growth, maturity, and service are all closely connected in verses 14–16.

Many people are reluctant to commit to regular service in their local church. Yet there comes a point in all our lives where service is required if we are going to grow. We not only need knowledge, we need to put that knowledge into practice in meaningful service. As you look for a church, look for a leadership team that is committed to lead you. The process will seem painful at times, but it yields good fruit. Athletes want to quit long before their coaches let them. The extra effort their coaches require is not to punish them, but to prepare them for the game.

Equipping also includes being a good example. Once again, the Bible encourages you to be equipped in a local church where you can see your leaders (and others) live godly lives in the midst of blessings and challenges (1 Timothy 4:12; 1 Thessalonians 1:7 explains that being a good example is not a calling that is limited to a pastor). Having positive, encouraging role models will help you respond in faith, courage, and obedience when difficulties occur in your own life. This does not mean that the pastors are supposed to look perfect on the outside. Everyone struggles; everyone goes through trials and difficulties. So look for leaders who rely on Christ for strength. Look for leaders who pray, read their Bibles, and look for grace to help in their time of need (Hebrews 4:16), who know it is possible that hurt and hope can live in the same person at the same time (Psalm 42:5). Being a good example is not just about doing the right things; it is about having a heart that is dependent on Christ.

Ephesians 4 makes it clear that this equipping has valuable benefits. Just as the coach's training regimen results in better conditioning, skills, and performance in his players, so the church's equipping results in believers who are more faithful followers of Jesus. The equipping results in genuine maturity. Instead of being susceptible to lies from our culture or your own mind, you will be grounded in the truth. You will see things for what they are and you will be able to anticipate where things are going. *Star Wars* came out when I was a child. (I still remember trick-or-treating as Luke Skywalker!) The Jedi had quick reflexes because they could see things before they happened. In a sense, that is what maturity is. It spots deception before its horrible consequences occur. Maturity is able to see with wisdom. This does not simply come with age. Believers mature as they are continuously equipped.

Here again these themes point us to the importance of having Jesus as our center. The maturity the Bible talks about is not simply the maturity of an older person, but the maturity exhibited by Jesus himself. In order for this to be present in you, Jesus must be at the center of your life.

Practically speaking, this means that you will go to church looking to be led and taught, and to be surrounded by good examples. Attending a local church is not a passive, consumer-minded endeavor. We are not to view the church the same way we view the place we go to lunch after church. We are to look for ways to be equipped. This may involve immersing yourself in teaching the church offers; it may involve volunteering for specific service opportunities; it may involve changing your schedule.

I have worked with young couples for a decade. Some of them prioritized camping, visiting family, and even sleeping an extra hour over being equipped spiritually. Unfortunately, the lack of equipping has resulted in a lack of Christian maturity. But I have seen other couples who want to be equipped, who want to be led, and who want to mature. Not surprisingly, these couples grew in their walk with Christ, became leaders in the church, and are enjoying the fruit of Christian maturity. I personally encourage young couples to view faithfulness to church as attending forty-eight out of fifty-two Sundays a year. This may mean that camping and family visits end on Saturday night. It may mean that Saturday night ends at 11 p.m. so that one is rested and ready for Sunday morning, as opposed to staying up until 2 a.m. and rolling into church like a zombie.

God designed the church to be the place where you would be encouraged to love and good deeds. He also designed it to be a place where you would be equipped so that you would experience the joys of maturity.

To Provide Others to Care for You

Brothers, if anyone is caught in any transgression,
you who are spiritual should restore him in a spirit
of gentleness. Keep watch on yourself, lest you too be
tempted. Bear one another's burdens, and so fulfill the

law of Christ. For if anyone thinks he is something, when he is nothing, he deceives himself. But let each one test his own work, and then his reason to boast will be in himself alone and not in his neighbor. For each will have to bear his own load. (Galatians 6:1–5)

Blessed be the God and Father of our Lord Jesus Christ, the Father of mercies and God of all comfort, who comforts us in all our affliction, so that we may be able to comfort those who are in any affliction, with the comfort with which we ourselves are comforted by God. (2 Corinthians 1:3–4)

For just as the body is one and has many members, and all the members of the body, though many, are one body, so it is with Christ. . . .The eye cannot say to the hand, "I have no need of you," nor again the head to the foot, "I have no need of you." (1 Corinthians 12:18, 21)

Galatians 6 and 2 Corinthians 1 remind us of the two core struggles we face as human beings made in the image of God: suffering and sin. As God instructed the church, he made it clear that ministry to one another addresses both of these struggles.

Let's consider the suffering side for a moment.

I mentioned that I have worked with young couples for a while. One common struggle they face is infertility. For reasons only God knows, some couples have a difficult time conceiving children. Can you imagine facing this struggle without anyone knowing or caring for you? Can you imagine being asked four hundred times when you are going to have children without someone else crying with you later? As a church we have had to learn how to care for people in this situation. Infertile couples have had to learn how to rejoice with couples that have children. Those with children have had to learn to be sensitive to those who cannot. All of us have matured by thinking about these things. That is the church in action. We don't just dispense biblical content. We are a community of caring people who seek to love those around us. We love by rejoicing when there is something worth celebrating and we love by weeping when there is something to cry about. Couples who hold back from being connected miss out on the care available to them in the body of Christ, and we miss out on what they could bring to us.

I do not pretend to know the ways in which God will allow you to suffer in the days ahead. But I do know that God uses his Word, his Spirit, and his church as means of help and comfort. Therefore, it is crucial to be part of the church.

Now let's consider the sin side.

Just because couples go through this book does not mean that they will never have a sinful argument. In the heat of a struggle, some of the truths that have been learned are not properly applied. Couples in this situation respond in different ways. Some pull out this book and re-read the material and review their notecards of Bible verses. Others allow moments like this to fester and produce bitterness that only results in more fighting. But almost all of the couples are helped if there is a godly person or couple that they can speak with.

Galatians 6:1–5 reminds us that there are spiritual people in the church who should be ready to help in moments just like this. They minister with gentleness rather than with condemnation or with guilt and shame. They help to bear your burdens so that your load is lighter for a time. Imagine it this way. When my daughter was four years old, we took her on a thirteen-mile hike in the mountains. It was a long, hard hike for all of us (our other children were eight and twelve), but there was only one way that my daughter could complete the hike: I carried her for ten miles. I purposely bore that additional burden to lighten the load for her legs. That is what spiritual people do with those they are trying to help—they take a portion of their load.

I cannot imagine going through life without the help the church provides and without the opportunities it offers. Jesus is building his church and the way he has constructed it is both for his glory and our good.

Before I close this chapter, it might be helpful to explain what it looks like to be part of a Christian community that functions in this way.

First, there is *loyalty*. These passages presuppose that each member of the body will be invested in the body to fulfill its role. We live in a day when people change churches almost as fast as they change their clothes. If the pastor says something they don't like, they leave. If a nursery worker observes an issue in their child and mentions it, the parents leave. If they don't feel right, they leave. It is certainly important to find a church where one can be equipped, willingly submit to the leadership, and enjoy fellowship, but we should not move on to another without serious reflection and self-examination. Without a measure of loyalty, commitment, and investment, personal growth and meaningful ministry to others do not happen.

Ministry takes place in the context of community and relationship. Whenever we move to a new community, we must begin again to get to know people and build relationships that foster trust, honesty, and caring. Without those relationships, meaningful ministry that addresses the real issues in our lives does not occur. If we are not careful, our lack of loyalty will lead to a skepticism and even cynicism about the church that will destroy us.

Second, there is *importance* and *value*. The 1 Corinthians 12 passage particularly emphasize that every member of the body is important. Physically, we know this to be true. Recently I ate some contaminated food, and even though those bacteria were small, they produced a reaction that dominated my life for the next eighteen hours. What appears insignificant is really important! But somehow, we do not remember this as it pertains to the church. The Bible teaches that each of us has a part to play in the ongoing growth of the church. My part, whatever it may be, is significant and important. Without me, the body cannot function at its best. The same is true for you. God gifted you with skills, talents, and abilities that are designed to function in his body. When you are not invested in a church, you are not employing your God-given gifts as he intended. When we don't honor the Lord with what he has entrusted to us, we are not living with Jesus at the center of our lives.

Third, there is *dependence.* Each part of the body is dependent on the others. This means that when I go to church, ready to serve in the ways God has gifted me, I am also dependent on everyone else in my church who has come for the same purpose. They need my ministry and I need theirs. Let me be more personal. Some people in our church almost seem to produce their own light. When they enter a room, the room is brighter, more encouraging, and warmer than before. I, unfortunately, am not the same way. When I enter a room, darkness dominates, gloom approaches, and ice crystals begin to form on the window sills. Okay, I am exaggerating . . . a little. My point is that I need to be around warm and encouraging people just as much as they need my teaching. We serve one another and are dependent on one another's ministry.

Here's another example. Children's ministries are not stepping-stones to greater opportunities. Those who faithfully and enthusiastically serve in children's ministry serve the Lord, the children, and their parents. As a parent, I love it when my children are involved with passionate, gifted children's ministry workers. They reinforce the teaching I am doing at home and speak truth into my children's lives. My family would miss so much if they were not present!

I encourage you to invest yourself in service to the church. I encourage you to enter its doors looking for ways to make a difference in another person's life. Whether you are a teacher, a mercy giver, an encourager, a giver, or a musician, your gifts are needed to help the church function properly.

I hope this chapter has awakened your passion for the local church. It is the place for equipping, for serving, and for receiving service from others. If you are unwilling to faithfully participate, you will experience a lack of Christian maturity and a loss of ministry opportunity. In contrast, a faithful and passionate investment in a local church will not only be a blessing to you, but to those around you.

Homework Discussion Questions

Complete the following questions on your own and then share your answers with your fiancé(e). Later, discuss your answers and your conversation as a couple with your mentor.

Think deeply about these questions. Shallow answers will hurt you and your future spouse more than anyone else. Deeper, more honest answers may lead to some uncomfortable moments, but that is okay. These real-life discussions will help you to prepare and learn as a couple.

1. Describe your church background.
   a. Where did you go as a child?
   b. How long have you been consistently attending your current church?
   c. How do you serve in the church?
   d. What role do you believe the church should play in your life after you are married?
2. What have you learned about the local church in this chapter?
3. What are your greatest fears or concerns about investing in the local church in the ways this chapter suggests?
4. What two statements in this chapter had the most impact on you? What struck you about them? Be prepared to discuss this as a couple and with your mentor.

5. Choose the Bible passage from this chapter that was most significant to you. Put it on an index card and review it daily until you meet with your mentor. You should now have seven passages of Scripture; one from each chapter.

6. What truths have you learned about Christ that would increase your appreciation for the local church and your involvement in it?

7. Why do you think a love for Jesus and a focus on the gospel are important when developing relationships and loyalty in a church family?

8. List two ways you need to change in light of this material. Where do you need to repent? How do you need God to help you?

9. Spend at least five minutes daily praying for yourself and your fiancé(e), that Jesus would be at the center of your lives and that you would love the church as much as Jesus does.

Advanced Homework

Here is an additional possibility for homework that couples may find helpful.

- Read *Church Membership* by Jonathan Leeman (Wheaton, IL: Crossway, 2012). This book explains the biblical reasons for church membership and why believers should demonstrate the loyalty and commitment involved in becoming official members of a local church.

Chapter 8

Intimacy with Jesus as the Center

IT MIGHT SEEM strange to have the words *Sex* and *Jesus* in the same sentence, whether you have grown up in the church or not! Either way, it's sometimes hard to fathom that your worship of the Lord Jesus has everything to do with the quality of your sex life in marriage. But if you are a believer, you have every reason to believe that your sex life can be enjoyable and fulfilling.

At the outset, though, we should acknowledge that you may be reading this book with very little knowledge of this aspect of life. By God's grace, you are innocent. You may even be a bit nervous about what you might find in this chapter. Let me assure you that you have nothing to fear. I believe that this material can be helpful, encouraging, and confidence-building as your honeymoon approaches. As we rely on the Lord, he will continually give us grace to live according to his Word, where he has given us a lot of instruction on marital intimacy.

Or perhaps you are someone who has had many sexual experiences. Some were positive and some you wish you could forget. No matter what your experience, let me encourage you to be a learner.

Let God's words on this subject shape—and reshape—your attitude. As you allow your mind to focus on the things that are truly biblical, you will be prepared for a God-honoring, enjoyable sex life with your spouse.

The Bible has a lot of say about sex. In fact, almost every book of the Bible teaches something about sex and intimacy. Sometimes people only know the passages that talk about the dangers of illicit sex, but the Bible has many positive things to say about sex as well. Sex within marriage is one of the ways we can honor and glorify the Lord, and it is designed to build and strengthen our marital relationship. We have every reason to look forward to a vibrant sex life if Jesus is at the center. No matter what your past history, a joyful, God-honoring experience is available to you.

Here is the key theme of this chapter: *Sex is not about performance; sex is about relationship.* You might try saying that to yourself about ten times.

Our society places an incredible, unrelenting emphasis on sexual performance. *Cosmopolitan's* long-running presence on the newsstand is evidence of that fascination. Though I have never read a single issue, its covers make me fully aware that the magazine offers sex tips in every issue. And enough people apparently buy them to keep the magazine in business. In addition, there are books without number dedicated to the topic, and even sex clinics throughout the country dedicated to helping people improve their sexual performance.

Scripture, however, is not as concerned about performance as it is concerned about relationship. Like every other area of life, our sex life must have the authentic and meaningful worship of Christ as its foundation. Let's see how Scripture speaks to this important matter.

God Created Sex for Procreation and Meaningful Relationship

> Therefore a man shall leave his father and his mother and hold fast to his wife, and they shall become one flesh. (Genesis 2:24)

Sex was God's idea. He could have created a world where procreation happened less personally—like the way a flower is pollinated. The Creator, however, designed a relationship in which one man and one woman would be joined in body and soul. God designed it so that each couple would leave their previous family unit and start a new one. The phrase "one flesh" may describe more than just sex, but it is certainly not less than sex. The marital union is meaningful, powerful, and so significant that it has priority over other family relationships.

Within this union is the creation command to be fruitful and fill the earth. This command is fulfilled through sexual relations,[4] but this is not the simple physical coupling of the animal world. Human intimacy involves a spiritual union as well. First Corinthians 6:19–20 explains, "Or do you not know that your body is a temple of the Holy Spirit within you, whom you have from God? You are not your own, for you were bought with a price. So glorify God in your body." The joining of two bodies into one has a spiritual dimension.

When God designed human sex, he wanted it to be about relationship, not about performance.

---

4. I realize that there are some couples who would love to have children but have not been able to do so. These are potentially significant issues. If you have fears about your ability to have children, please speak with your mentor.

God Created Sex to Be Enjoyed within a Monogamous Marriage; All Other Forms Are Wrong

The fact that God restricted sex to the marriage covenant is further evidence that God designed human sex to be about relationship. Even though God designed sex to be pleasurable, he did not want two people to have sex simply because they found each other attractive. Proving that all forms of sexuality outside the boundaries of monogamous marriage are forbidden is fairly easy in the Bible. Consider these two passages:

> Finally, then, brothers, we ask and urge you in the Lord Jesus, that as you received from us how you ought to walk and to please God, just as you are doing, that you do so more and more. For you know what instructions we gave you through the Lord Jesus. For this is the will of God, your sanctification: that you abstain from sexual immorality; that each one of you know how to control his own body in holiness and honor, not in the passion of lust like the Gentiles who do not know God. (1 Thessalonians 4:1–5)

> Drink water from your own cistern, flowing water from your own well. Should your springs be scattered abroad, streams of water in the streets? Let them be for yourself alone, and not for strangers with you. Let your fountain be blessed, and rejoice in the wife of your youth, a lovely deer, a graceful doe. Let her breasts fill you at all times with delight; be intoxicated always in her love. (Proverbs 5:15–19)

If you have had previous sexual experiences, it is important to re-train your mind and to remember that God's will is that all forms of immorality are to be forever absent from your relationship. (The "water" in Proverbs 5 has nothing to do with the well in your backyard, as the rest of the passage makes clear.)

Thus, all forms of pornography, masturbation, adultery, or other types of immorality must be removed from your relationship. Failure to do so will not only result in relationship pain, it may result in the loss of the relationship altogether. Most importantly, it will not display the glory of God. If you are struggling with your physical relationship or if there is a pattern of pornography and/or masturbation, it is important to discuss this with your mentor.

At the same time, these passages present some wonderful ideals for marital intimacy. First, it is by God's grace that we can live in such a way that our bodies are used for holy and honorable purposes. Outside of marriage this looks like abstinence, but inside marriage it looks like intoxicating love (as we see at the end of the Proverbs passage). Second, words and phrases like "sanctification," "will of God," "blessed," "rejoiced" all describe the great joy that is possible when sex is experienced in marriage as God intended.

A husband looks at his wife

The boundaries God sets for sexual relationships in no way contradict the fact that God created sex to be enjoyed. This truth is clearly taught in the Song of Solomon. Over the centuries, people have interpreted the Song in different ways. Some have seen it as a metaphor for the relationship between Christ and the church; some suggest that it presents the progression from dating to wedding to honeymoon. I believe the Song (songs, actually) describes the marriage relationship. The songs overlap in their teaching and reinforce similar ideas. One of the songs' most obvious emphases is the enjoyment associated with sex. Speeches by the wife about her husband and the husband about his wife capture the essence of their mutual enjoyment. Here is one example:

How beautiful are your feet in sandals, O noble daughter! Your rounded thighs are like jewels, the work of a master hand. Your navel is a rounded bowl that never lacks mixed wine. Your belly is a heap of wheat, encircled with lilies. Your two breasts are like two fawns, twins of a gazelle. Your neck is like an ivory tower. Your eyes are pools in Heshbon, by the gate of Bath-rabbim. Your nose is like a tower of Lebanon, which looks toward Damascus. Your head crowns you like Carmel, and your flowing locks are like purple; a king is held captive in the tresses. How beautiful and pleasant you are, O loved one, with all your delights! Your stature is like a palm tree, and your breasts are like its clusters. I say I will climb the palm tree and lay hold of its fruit. Oh may your breasts be like clusters of the vine, and the scent of your breath like apples, and your mouth like the best wine. It goes down smoothly for my beloved, gliding over lips and teeth. (Song of Solomon 7:1–9)

Admittedly, the wise husband of today will not simply repeat these words verbatim to his bride! I don't think the average modern woman would appreciate having her belly equated to a heap of wheat (v. 2), or her nose to a tower (v. 4), or her head to a mountain (v. 5). However, each of these images pointed to a significant reality. What the man really says about his wife can be summarized in a few points.

1. She is perfect. She is the work of a master craftsman. He describes almost every part of her body in a complimentary fashion. While the argument cannot be fully developed here, it appears that not everyone has the same opinion of her. In other words, she doesn't seem to have what society considered to be the perfect body. However, in the mind of her beloved, she is perfect. The man has redefined beauty within the loving relationship he has with his bride.

2. She is intoxicating. When the bridegroom says that she has a navel never lacking mixed wine and a belly that is encircled with lilies, he is saying that he is intoxicated with her body. It overpowers, controls, and completely satisfies him. The bride is not left wondering whether her man thinks she is too fat, too ugly, too small, or too flabby. He is making it clear that what she brings to him is more than he can handle. To put it slightly differently, this man is drunk with his bride's body.

3. She is beautiful. Whether he is speaking of her breasts, her neck, her hair, or her eyes, he describes something beautiful and wonderful. His willingness to talk about all of her indicates that he notices and enjoys every aspect of her. This is not about how she would rank in a beauty contest evaluated by a hundred men. This is an expression of what one man sees in his bride.

While some of the actual comparisons are a bit confusing, it is clear that this man intensely desires his bride and she satisfies him completely. This kind of passion is not found in magazines, it is found in a loving, covenant relationship with one's beloved. After all, sex is not about performance; it is about relationship.

All too often, we are stuck in the world's definition of beauty— or worse, we are stuck in a fantasy world of beauty. Men seem to be particularly vulnerable here. Men, please see that God wants you to define beauty by the picture of your bride. The more you see her through the lens of knowing that God created her to be entirely satisfying to you, the less you will be tempted to look elsewhere and the less you will wonder if there is anything better out there.

This brings us back to the point I have been making all along— Jesus must be at the center of every aspect of your life. I want to encourage men in particular to take the lead in ensuring that your sexual relationship will be pursued in a way that is consistent with the promises of Scripture. Ask God to work in your heart and mind to help you see your bride as perfect, beautiful, and intoxicating.

A wife looks at her husband

Since sex is between two people, both persons must think biblically about sex. According to Scripture, the woman should not be a passive participant. Just as Solomon makes a speech about his bride, so his bride makes a speech about him.

> My beloved is radiant and ruddy, distinguished among ten thousand. His head is the finest gold; his locks are wavy, black as a raven. His eyes are like doves beside streams of water, bathed in milk, sitting beside a full pool. His cheeks are like beds of spices, mounds of sweet-smelling herbs. His lips are lilies, dripping liquid myrrh. His arms are rods of gold, set with jewels. His body is polished ivory, bedecked with sapphires. His legs are alabaster columns, set on bases of gold. His appearance is like Lebanon, choice as the cedars. His mouth is most sweet, and he is altogether desirable. This is my beloved and this is my friend, O daughters of Jerusalem. (Song of Solomon 5:10–16)

Just as the wise husband will refrain from using the text verbatim, so will the wife. Some of the imagery found in the text is a bit odd for our day. But once we get past some of the imagery, we find some very important truths about the bride's view of her husband.

1. In her eyes, he is handsome. In verse 10 she calls him "radiant" and "ruddy." We don't normally think of men in those terms, but "handsome" seems to be a good modern counterpart. She says that his head is like pure gold, he has gorgeous eyes, and he has nice cheekbones. She believes her man is one handsome man! Think about how significant that is in a relationship. If sex takes place within marriage, as it should, the man wants to be desired. He is not hiring a hooker to give him pleasure. Your future husband will find pleasure in the reality that you find him attractive and that you want to be intimate with him. In my counseling experience, one of the greatest sexual frustrations among men is that they don't feel very wanted. They believe their wife is a passive, willing-but-less-than-enthusiastic participant. After a while, that gets old! Let me encourage you to learn a lesson from this passage: desire your handsome husband.

2. In her eyes, he is well-built. She speaks of his arms as strong and his core as if it is polished ivory. She says that his legs are like pillars, again referring to a strong and muscular look. If this is Solomon, I must admit that I struggle viewing Solomon as a well-built man. Unlike his father David, who beat the tar out of every challenger, Solomon gets others to do the fighting for him. While I am exercising a sanctified imagination (and maybe not all that sanctified!), I tend to think that Solomon was probably no rock-hard, muscle-bulging dude on the cover of the ancient equivalent of the *Men's Health* magazine. I suspect his activity level and diet during his tremendously prosperous reign would have put him in the more normal modern-day American category. But I think this bride is doing just what her husband did—they make each other the standard of beauty. Now, I am not suggesting that ladies lie! Your man may not have that ivory chest. And his six-pack may still be stuck in the cooler! But performance is not the point; relationship is. From this wife's perspective, he is just right.

3. In her eyes, he is the best of ten thousand. I personally find her comment, "distinguished among ten thousand," to be the most significant and sexiest of all. Many of us men would put ourselves in the "average" category. We are okay-looking, but we're not going to be asked to advertise popular products or appear on magazine covers. We are just a bunch of average guys. The picture this bride paints is that her husband is so awesome that, if she had a choice of any one of ten thousand men, she would still pick her man! I know for a fact that if ten thousand men were lined up, my wife could find someone smarter, richer, better looking, more fun, with a better body, etc., etc. But the fact that she would choose me would be a statement of love and loyalty. That is the kind of heart the Lord wants you to have for your future husband.

4. *In her eyes, he is wholly desirable.* The bride ends her speech by saying that her bridegroom is wholly desirable. That is a very sexy and attractive way to talk about your husband! Most husbands would love to hear their wives say things like that. It is very wise to start your marriage building this kind of relationship.

There may be some who think I am saying that sex is the most vital part of marriage. I don't believe that's what Scripture teaches. However, sex and intimacy are important parts of marriage. They are one way that marriages can be strengthened and, sadly, one way that marriages can be destroyed. Scripture is clear that, while sex is not first about performance, there can be great enjoyment in your sexual intimacy because that is the way God designed it.

God Designed Sex for Mutual Benefit, with a Focus on Pleasing One's Spouse

> Now concerning the matters about which you wrote: "It is good for a man not to have sexual relations with a woman." But because of the temptation to sexual immorality, each man should have his own wife and each woman her own husband. The husband should

give to his wife her conjugal rights, and likewise the wife to her husband. For the wife does not have authority over her own body, but the husband does. Likewise the husband does not have authority over his own body, but the wife does. Do not deprive one another, except perhaps by agreement for a limited time, that you may devote yourselves to prayer; but then come together again, so that Satan may not tempt you because of your lack of self-control. (1 Corinthians 7:1–5)

This passage outlines the responsibility that spouses have to each other. While duty is certainly not the primary motivation for sexual relations, this passage indicates that duty is a possible motivation. It is also clear that God gives each spouse some level of ownership over the other person's body. We should not push this analogy too far, for we know that both persons first and foremost belong to the Lord. There is no support in this passage for abusive behavior. However, laying the extremes aside, the text is clear that when you are married, you belong to each other. The importance of regular sexual relations can be seen in Paul's statement that sexual intimacy should only be postponed for the purpose of devoted prayer. The time of postponement is to be relatively short so that neither person is willfully placed in the place of temptation.

These truths have some tremendous implications.

First, all sexual behavior outside of marriage violates these truths and trains the person to think about sex in an unbiblical way. Pornography and masturbation are examples of self-gratification; those who engage in them train themselves for self-pleasure. These behaviors also train a person to respond to certain images and certain forms of touch. Sadly, these habits do not disappear on the wedding day, and sex after marriage is influenced by them. The truths about duties and ownership found in this passage make it clear that sex is intended for mutual benefit. But sexual experiences erode rapidly if one spouse believes he or she is merely being used.

Second, it is important to guard against manipulating your spouse with or for sex. This happens with both men and women. Women may promise sex if their husbands help with the children or with household chores. They may consent to sex only because of their intense desire for a baby (not for their husbands), so that sex becomes the means to the end of pregnancy. Men, on the other hand, manipulate their wives by telling them that they will be less tempted if they have regular sex. There are, of course, elements of truth to these manipulations. It is true that sex is a prerequisite to pregnancy and it is true that regular sexual activity is one aid in fighting temptation. But when couples speak honestly, the heart of manipulation becomes clearer. Manipulation erodes trust and may eventually erode the relationship.

Third, sex is one of the ways you serve your spouse rather than use him or her. In the counseling office, my colleagues and I have heard about the following statements made on the honeymoon: "I wish you had lost another twenty pounds"; "That lingerie was not very attractive"; "Sex was not as good as I thought it would be"; "Yes, I texted my friends after our first night"; "Why can't you control yourself for two whole minutes?" In each of these cases, serious damage was done to the relationship because one partner was defining sex through the grid of performance and self-gratification rather than relationship, the covenant that was just established, and the union confirmed in heaven.

Your sexual relationship is a journey. If you see how your relationship with God impacts the way you think about sex, then your most enjoyable sexual experiences will not be on your honeymoon. Instead, as you grow in your love and care for the Lord and each other over time, your sex life will become more enjoyable, more relationship-building, and more tender than you can ever imagine.

Enjoy every step of the way! When I see couples argue and hurt each other through sex, I am sad that they have missed out on one of the great blessings God designed for us. Please set your heart and mind on Christ and enjoy whatever God allows.

What about the Honeymoon?

Some couples are nervous about the honeymoon. Most have certain expectations for how the honeymoon should go and they are afraid they may not live up to them. Let me encourage you that what we have just considered can help you by eliminating all such preconceived notions and expectations. Weddings are stressful events, with many things to do, many people to organize, and many things that are simply outside your control. This means that couples begin their honeymoon after a couple of very stressful days, which is not exactly the time when people are at their best. When you add nervousness, awkwardness, or certain expectations about sex to the mix, you have the ingredients for relationship damage.

Instead, set aside your expectations and concentrate on enjoying the journey together. You don't have to meet certain performance standards; you have the opportunity to love Jesus and each other by focusing on the relationship. So don't focus on what each of you will wear, or what you will do, or how much money you are spending for the first night. Choose to enjoy each other's companionship and, yes, even the awkwardness. After all, honeymoon sex will not be your best sex anyway. And remember, sex is not about performance, but about relationship. The stronger the bond you establish and the more years of togetherness you have, the better the sex can become.

What about Preferences?

Most of the couples I have counseled through the years want to please the other person (at least they say they do). Thus, they ask each other what types of things they would enjoy. When both agree on these preferences, couples are free to move forward. What happens, however, when one person is not comfortable? Awkwardness occurs because, on the one hand, both people want to serve. On the other hand, both people want what they want!

There is a way out of this impasse. Not surprisingly, it involves Christ at the center.

Step 1: Think carefully about the experiences of your spouse

If we really knew each other's stories, we might be a bit surprised by what we find. You may be someone who would say that you had very healthy relationships with the opposite sex. You did not compromise Scripture, you will get married as a virgin, and you did not spend your teens asking "How far can I go?" You sought to honor God with your body.

Then again, you might be someone who would say that you had sexual experience(s) prior to marriage, including a date rape. The person took advantage of you and everything he did was repulsive to you.

Others come to marriage after living an "anything goes" life before meeting Jesus. You were exposed to a world your spouse may know nothing about.

It isn't hard to imagine the challenges that can arise as people with such different pasts marry. Begin by simply being patient. If your spouse has always been sexually conservative, it is unwise to suggest positions or activities that would make your spouse uncomfortable. It would be even more troublesome and inconsiderate if you were irritated with your spouse for not being interested in those things.

Step 2: Clearly communicate your preferences (positively or negatively)

You need to communicate clearly. If certain things seem wicked to you, communicate that. Our world has pushed all kinds of sexual ideas into our minds, but that does not necessarily mean we must adopt them.

So communicate your preferences, but at this stage that is all you are doing. If you had many sexual experiences before your marriage, you will need to be particularly cautious. You do not want to sound like you are comparing your wife to the other women in your life (or your husband to other men). If you do this regularly, don't be surprised if your sex life and marriage rapidly deteriorate. Your spouse won't want to be compared to all the others.

Step 3: Willingly and joyfully give up your preferences rather than force your will

Sometimes the first two steps of thinking carefully and communicating clearly are enough to resolve any differences. But what if you are still at an impasse? Space does not allow me to develop the full argument of 1 Corinthians 8–10 but, basically, these chapters explain that we should be willing to give up our preferences if that results in encouragement and Christian growth in the other person.

Paul explains in 8:11–13 that even though idols are nothing, he would not eat meat offered to idols if his eating created a spiritual burden for others. In 9:1–7, and 15, Paul explains that he has a right to many things, but he chooses not to demand or exercise those rights. Instead, he has cultivated a heart attitude that focuses on service, compassion, and care for others. That perspective will serve couples well in the bedroom too.

I am convinced that if you push, you will be able to get your way a number of times. But have you ever considered how God might feel, knowing that you were so insensitive to one of his children?

Summary

God created sex to be enjoyed in the bonds of marriage. It is an expression of his divine will, not only for purposes of procreation, but of enjoyment. The Bible explains that sex is a loving expression of the covenant made between a man and a woman to be life partners. Biblical sex redefines the concept of beauty. Biblical sex redefines the concept of closeness, safety, and security in each other's arms. By God's grace, you will have a lifetime together to grow, develop, explore, and appreciate each other. So be patient, enjoy the journey, and celebrate the goodness and graciousness of a loving God who designed you for this.

Homework Discussion Questions

Complete the following questions on your own and then share your answers with your fiancé(e). Later, discuss your answers and your conversation as a couple with your mentor.

Think deeply about these questions. Shallow answers will hurt you and your future spouse more than anyone else. Deeper, more honest answers may lead to some uncomfortable moments, but that is okay. These real-life discussions will help you to prepare and learn as a couple.

1. What fears or concerns do you have concerning the sexual aspect of your marriage? The fears could come from past personal experiences or the lack of experience.
2. What safeguards have you put in place to ensure that you don't create unhelpful expectations for your honeymoon?
3. Explain the statement "Sex is not about performance, it is about relationship" in your own words.
4. What are your thoughts about contraceptives?

5. What two statements in this chapter had the most impact on you? Why? Be prepared to discuss this as a couple and with your mentor.

6. Which Bible passage was most significant to you? Write it on an index card and review it each day until your appointment with your mentor.

7. What truths have you learned about Christ that encourage you to allow Jesus to influence your sex life?

8. Explain why depending on Christ and remembering all the promises he has made to you would be important in developing a God-pleasing sex life with your spouse.

9. Spend at least five minutes daily praying for yourself and your future spouse, that Jesus would truly be the center of your life and that your sex life would bring Jesus glory and honor.

Advanced Homework

Here is an additional homework possibility that couples may find encouraging and beneficial.

- Read *Sex, Romance, and Glory of God* by C. J. Mahaney (Wheaton, IL: Crossway, 2004). This book explains how sexual intimacy within marriage brings glory to God when each spouse has the right heart attitude toward the other.

Conclusion

YOU ARE ABOUT to embark on an amazing journey. God, in his wisdom, decided it was best for us to enjoy lifelong companionship in the bonds of marriage. It was also God's plan that we love him first. That is why each chapter in this book has attempted to show what it means to have Jesus at the center in every area of married life. Your relationship with Christ will impact every aspect of your relationship with your spouse. Jesus will sustain you, comfort you, strengthen you, and motivate you to live your life in a way that reflects his love, mercy, wisdom and power. As you confess your weaknesses and sins to him and receive his forgiveness and strength, he will enable your marriage to reflect the relationship between Christ and his church. Your relationship with Jesus will encourage you to come to him when your attitudes need to change. When couples find all that they need in Jesus and his saving work on their behalf, they will not be manipulative, demanding, demeaning, or controlling with each other. The great secret of a successful marriage is this: It is more about your love for Christ than it is about your compatibility as a couple.

The exercises you've worked on provided information that enabled your mentor to help you, but the most important thing was that, as a couple, you learned about each other. Please do not ignore those lessons. Keep this book and review the key truths from

Scripture and the new things you learned about each other. Your answers could be a great help to you as you build your life together.

So, with a mind full of Scripture and a heart that worships and relies on Jesus, enter this new stage of life together with hope, joy, and excitement. The Lord will be there to help you!

Appendix
Just for the Mentors

MENTORING A YOUNG couple is a wonderful privilege. The Lord is giving you the chance to help them to thrive and not just survive as they enter married life. This appendix offers specific comments about how to help a couple work through the themes of each chapter. But first, let me offer some general advice on mentoring an engaged couple.

First, I have written this book from a Christian perspective, using language and concepts that may be unfamiliar to an unbeliever who contacted you for help. Thus, to use this resource evangelistically, you may need to slow the pace to explain more concepts as you go. Perhaps you'll propose an initial meeting to explain their need for Christ as individuals and the value of beginning their marriage with him at the center. God may have more planned than either you or the couple could possibly have imagined. Please pray for your couple and be sensitive to the Spirit's leading.

Second, it's important to encourage your couple through the mentoring process, but you also have to be willing to push them. Few couples come with delusions of grandeur for marriage but most come without the maturity in Christ or in human relationships to anticipate potential struggles. In the state where I live (Indiana), young people must drive fifty hours with their permit before they can get a license. Our state maintains that when young people begin driving, they are not fully aware of their surroundings and are prone to making mistakes. In marriage, however, there is no trial period. They say "I do" and off they go. Few couples come with the self-awareness and relationship awareness it takes to develop strong marriages from the beginning. Your job is to help them see what they are not seeing (much like a person who is learning to drive). Your job is to challenge them in areas where they didn't even know there was a challenge.

Third, you have to be willing to tell the couple your thoughts. I have, on occasion, had to tell a couple that I could not in good conscience officiate at their wedding. As a mentor, it is not necessarily your duty to marry the couple. Your job is to shepherd them. While they may not see it at first, the most loving thing you can do is tell the couple if you do not believe they are ready for marriage. We must avoid making rash judgments, of course. However, I can name many people who should never have married. If their mentor had made that clear, so much sin, hurt, pain, and disgrace to the name of Christ could have been avoided.

Fourth, you are their greatest cheerleader. Yes, you are willing to talk about the hard things, but you are also the one who wants to see them succeed by God's grace. I like to tell our couples that I am their biggest fan. I will experience great joy in watching the Lord work so that their marriage is all that God intended. So celebrate when you see them take Christ's Word seriously. Applaud them as they make discoveries about themselves or about their fiancé(e). Every time I have done premarital counseling, it has involved some degree of tension. There have been a few hard conversations with each couple. However, there has also been great joy as I have watched them grow and mature before my eyes.

Fifth, you should have no other stake in this matter than the one that represents the Lord Jesus. You must commit that your counsel to this couple will not rely on your experience, but on the Word of the Lord. Thus, you will be consistently pointing them to their relationship with Jesus as Savior and Lord. As Savior, the cross is the place of Jesus's suffering; as Lord, heaven is his abode. Suffering and humility characterized his first coming; rule and sovereignty will characterize his second coming. Jesus is at the center of every chapter because your couple's relationship with the risen Jesus should impact every area of their lives. Five years from now, you can count your ministry to them a success if they remember that every session was focused on Christ and the ways a meaningful relationship with Christ would make marriage better.

Sixth, this book deals with the major topics couples must address in marriage. However, some couples face specific challenges or special circumstances that go beyond these themes. For example, I spent more time working on parenting issues with one couple than I did on all the material in this book. The bride was entering the marriage with a young child from a previous relationship. Her fiancé not only needed to learn how to be a dad to this little boy, he also needed to understand how the biological father's relationship with his son would impact his marriage. This book can't cover all possible scenarios, so if your couple is dealing with an issue like this, consider involving additional people who can offer wise counsel. This material can be adjusted to allow other issues to be addressed. Feel free to take the time that's needed to help them. There are eight chapters, but that doesn't mean that premarital counseling must last only eight sessions.

Seventh, it isn't necessary to cover every question in each chapter with your couple. The assignments are designed to help them think and practice Christ-centered living. A couple that attempts to answer the questions thoughtfully is already accomplishing that goal. My hope is that their answers will be a resource for them as they begin married life. Take time to cover the questions you believe are most relevant to their specific issues. I generally spend about one hour each week with the couple and I typically cover three or four questions in detail. I give the couple an opportunity to ask questions and then I give a brief preview of the next chapter.

What follows is intended to help you understand how the chapters are organized and how I like to use them in my counseling.

Chapter 1

Right from the start, I want to help the couple see that their horizontal relationship with each other is dependent on their vertical relationship with the Lord. Issues of worship, love for Christ, commitment to the Word, and living obediently for God's honor and glory are absolutely essential for a Christ-centered marriage. However, most couples come to the counseling session thinking that their marriage is about a list of rules and practices to follow. In reality, building a marriage involves so much more than that.

As I talk with the couple, I look for a history of love and worship for God that existed before the couple's relationship. In other words, I don't want the guy to be serious about Jesus only because his fiancée is serious about Jesus. That motivation tends to dissipate after the wedding. While I don't expect spiritual giants to walk into the room, we as mentors have a "yellow flag" reason for concern if there is not a track record of godliness prior to their relationship. I often use little diagrams to illustrate this point. On the first diagram are lines that connect each person to Jesus.

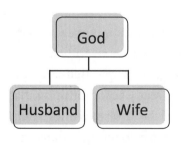

The second diagram shows the wife pointing to the husband who is pointed to Christ.

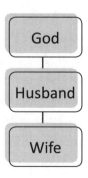

With these diagrams, I hope to show the couple that there is only one Mediator between God and man, and that is Christ. If a man is leading his wife well, she will become more in love with Jesus and thus rely on Jesus to provide her greatest needs, and the husband will experience the joys of being married to a happy woman. Similarly, a wife cannot be the mediator between God and her husband. Too often men have seen their own walk with God through their relationship with their wife. A more biblical understanding is that each spouse must have his or her own vibrant and meaningful walk with God. A second-hand attachment to Jesus is a clear sign that the relationship has potential issues.

I also look to see who is more spiritually mature. Who, for example, would be quicker to run to sin? My point is not to demean anyone, but to encourage an honest self-awareness of their commitment to Christ in the ten thousand little moments of life. Life is lived in very small moments, where the identity of our true love and object of worship is displayed. I am not satisfied unless the couple is able to explain their own commitment to Christ in the little moments of life (e.g., on Sunday morning, with their physical standards, in the way they relate to each other, etc.). Thus, I often talk to my couples about "come to Jesus moments." These are the moments when I need to have a private conversation with Christ. Maybe I am hurt, angry, worried, or discouraged. While some of these moments may involve the other person, others are simply due to my own selfish idolatry. If couples can learn that there will be many "come to Jesus moments" in life, they will learn how to face their sins, repent, receive Christ's forgiveness, cleansing, and strength in ways that make life infinitely more satisfying than they ever imagined.

This chapter also establishes that a man is not going to be a Christian husband, a Christian employee, or a Christian father if he is not first a committed Christian. The same is true for the woman.

If my couples see their need to rely on the work of Jesus by having regular "come to Jesus" moments, actively pursuing Christ, and remembering that they can't be a Christian spouse or parent unless they are committed Christians, I have accomplished my goals for the first week.

Chapter 2

This chapter focuses on the biblical definition of love. After preaching a series on biblical love from 1 Corinthians 13 some time ago, I was so convicted that I wasn't sure I had ever loved anyone in my whole life! That was exactly the right conclusion. It placed me in a position of dependence. It made me realize that unless I am relying on Christ and his love for me, I will never live out the command to love biblically.

All too often, engaged couples think they love each other. They think there is hardly any room for improvement. In my experience, couples often list themselves as a 7 or 8 on the love scale, but that is for humility's sake. If the truth were told, they probably think of themselves as a 9 or 10. In reality, they are probably more like a 3. They are so blinded by the excitement of marriage that they do not see where they fall short. This is a place of pride. It may not stem from a rebellious heart (more like an ignorant one), but this pride will soon create challenges. I want my couples to see that they are just starting the journey to biblical love. Thus, I hope they will commit to praying even more fervently for their love to genuinely grow.

One way I try to enter into this conversation is through question #2. It asks each person to rate, on a scale of 1–10, how loving they are, biblically speaking. The purpose of the question is not to delineate the difference between a 5 or a 7 or an 8. The point is to get the couple talking about why they gave themselves that number and how they demonstrate that level of biblical love. Most importantly, I want to see whether they know the specific steps they need to take to grow in biblical love. The more I hear them express humility, dependence, and concern about being able to do this, the more relational maturity they have.

As they examine the true state of their hearts, I want them to wrestle with the possibility that they may want to marry their fiancé(e) not because they love them, but because they love themselves. The more they can move to a dependence on the Lord for biblical love, the stronger their relationship with each other will be.

Chapter 3

I include a chapter on problem solving early in the book for two reasons. First, when couples refuse to live for Christ, their own sinfulness will create problems. I like to tell my couples, "When you do not function according to chapters 1 and 2, you will need chapter 3."

The second reason this chapter comes early is because I don't know anyone who has lived a problem-free life! Even if couples are doing a really great job of living for Christ and keeping their self-created problems to a minimum, problems sometimes originate externally. The loss of a job, financial pressures, or parents who seek to control their married children can create an environment where problems can grow.

That's why every couple must learn how to solve problems. I don't necessarily want to emphasize problems, but I want to see that the couple can biblically solve one. This is such a concern for me that, if I do not see a genuine understanding and practice of biblical problem solving, I question whether the wedding should take place or whether I should be involved.

I want the couple to be able to explain the four steps of problem solving and to show how they implemented those steps in particular instances. This chapter may require two weeks to cover, especially if the couple is unsure about the process.

When covering this chapter I look for several things. First, I want to see that the couple understands that there is a difference between "asking for forgiveness" and repentance. After all, it is possible to ask for forgiveness without a heart of repentance. Such action is hypocritical and leads to long-term bitterness.

Second, I want to see each person taking responsibility for his or her part in a problem. So often couples begin with confrontation, but in Scripture, problem solving begins when each person is willing to consider the log in his own eye. Couples who blame-shift are not only disobeying the Lord, they are setting a very dangerous precedent in their relationship.

Third, I look for spiritual maturity and wisdom in the way they approach problems. Here's a story to illustrate what I mean. I counseled a married couple after they had a physical altercation. The woman was nagging her husband and he completely lost control. He shoved her down the hall and slammed her into a wall. His attitude was, "If she had not nagged me, there wouldn't have been a physical altercation." In a very limited sense, he was right. There would not have been a physical altercation *that day*. He might also be correct that she needs to repent for the way she used her tongue. However—and this is a *big* however—with those words he is blaming her. He is not taking responsibility for his part in the fight, which was physically violent and completely unacceptable. This is not biblical repentance.

Some couples struggle with the order of Matthew 7. They want the speck and the log to come out at the exact same time, as both spouses confess their sin simultaneously. But Matthew 7 teaches that each person must BEGIN with the way he or she was at fault. The text is clear that the log must be removed first. This man needed to see that the event was his fault and to biblically repent without blaming his wife. Then, and only then, is it appropriate to speak to the wife about her tongue. Frankly, understanding and accepting what Matthew 7 really asks of us can be hard to grasp in the heat of the moment. But if a couple cannot demonstrate a measure of maturity at this level, I have concerns about how they will relate to each other in the future.

Fourth, I want to know if the couple understands the difference between trust and "moving forward." Sometimes one person really hurts the other. For example, the guy looks at pornography. His wife can forgive him and move forward but that does not necessarily mean she has full trust in him. If he equates forgiveness and trust, he will be very frustrated (wrongly so) with her whenever she is suspicious of further activity. She, in turn, will likely question the depth and sincerity of his repentance. Obviously, this atmosphere can lead to further difficulties. I want to help the couple understand the difference between forgiveness and trust so they are prepared to handle those hard moments should they come. She can forgive and still ask him to give up his computer use. She can forgive him and still request software like Covenant Eyes.

It should be clear that these four concepts require Jesus to be the center of each person's life. If the couple is not worshiping Christ, these will be challenging concepts to grasp.

Chapter 4

By the time the couple reaches chapter 4, we have often had some really intense—sometimes intimidating—conversations. Asking about a track record of godliness, helping them see that biblical love requires dependence on Christ, and talking about biblical problem solving often leaves a couple thankful for the lessons, but more aware that they are not living a fairy tale. In fact, the vast majority of my couples have been grateful to be taken to the cross every week, while also expressing that counseling is much harder than they had anticipated. So at this point we transition to a couple of topics that they might find a bit easier to talk about. Think of it this way: In athletics you cannot ask your team to practice at 100 percent of their effort every day. Instead, you have times of intensity and times of rest. The first three weeks are very intense because we talk about subjects that kill our pride and show us how weak we are. This week, we lighten up just a bit.

Chapter 4 is dedicated to two basic propositions. The first is that, while there are many duties involved in making a household work, there are only a few requirements given by the Lord. Couples often go through a transition period as they move from engagement to marriage. People often tell them about how hard it is. I think that advice is unhelpful. The fact that God requires only a few things is actually a freeing and encouraging thought. It says that you do not have to solve every issue on Day One. You can, as I like to say, "enjoy the adventure." If the couple will commit to being what God wants them to be in their marriage, it will free them to organize the rest of their lives in whatever way they desire. They have the freedom to experiment with how life could work and to enjoy discovering how best to function as a couple. In other words, there does not have to be a hard transition period. Instead, the transition to living as a couple can be fun!

The second proposition is that Christ serves as the example for every role given to the husband and the wife. I want couples to see that they are dependent on Christ in order to live out their role. This reinforces everything we covered in the first three chapters and keeps our focus on Christ's love for them, their love for Christ, and the empowerment of the Holy Spirit. Without these things, living out their God-given roles will be impossible.

If I have time, I briefly ask about how their household will run (finances, laundry, shopping, cleaning, etc.). However, if they embrace the two basic propositions, they will figure out the rest with minimal difficulty. If they fail to understand and apply the first two propositions, talking about the details is unlikely be of much value. It would be akin to framing a house without first putting down the foundation.

Chapter 5

We spent time on problem solving in chapter 3, so the focus of this chapter is more generally on how a couple should communicate.

To do that, I believe it is important to help the couple understand that communication flows from the heart—always. For that reason, giving couples rules or guidelines about communication is not very helpful until they understand that their communication will arise from what they want, not from what rules they know. The motivations and desires are different for each person. Some like to be viewed as right; they cannot stand to "agree to disagree." Others like to be viewed as important, which is why multitasking during a conversation is simply unacceptable. Possible desires and motivations are quite varied, so it is important to help a couple see their own. This information is useful to you as a mentor, but it is crucial for the couple. I want to be aware of potential trouble spots, but I am far more concerned that the couple is self-aware.

It's possible that your couple will need to be taught to repent of a ruling desire. It is easy to see how idolatry is the source of ungodly speech. This truth points us again to the significance of our walk with Christ. I want my couples to hear me say over and over and over again that the quality of their marriage will be based on the quality of their walk with Christ.

Once they understand how their hearts influence their communication, the focus is on positive ways to communicate. Ephesians 4:29 not only commands us to not speak unwholesome words, it more importantly commands us to speak words that build up or edify. So many couples fail to offer each other encouragement or kind words. The longer they are married, the more time they spend talking about problems. I want to help couples to begin their marriage seeing the importance of honesty, keeping short accounts, offering regular encouragement, and choosing kindness in their speech. The more they think about using their tongue to build rela-tionships, the better. This will not only help them honor the Lord, it will result in a blessed marriage relationship as well.

Chapter 6

Many young people have been taught very little about finances, and much of what has been written is good advice but not neces-sarily Christ-centered. It is simply common sense. God calls us to something far more. I want my couples to exhibit an understand-ing of the heart issues involved in finances. This does not consist of following simple rules. Instead, there is a wrestling with ten-sions between giving and planning, between giving and enjoying what God has given, between contentment and planning. It means dealing with the heart issues involved when there are competing priorities. This requires us to be dependent on the Lord. We must live in humility, depending on Christ for all our financial decisions. I hope that this brief discussion will lead couples to do more study in the future. For example, due to space constraints, I did not dis-cuss debt. However, discussing finances may take more than one week, especially if your couple needs a session dedicated to a dis-cussion on debt.

I chose to focus this chapter on issues of the heart, but I know that numbers eventually need to be put on a page. I encourage you to evaluate their first year's budget and offer some ways to help them honor Christ. If they will ask the right questions, you have helped them. For example, you could ask the couple, "Do you believe that the amount of money you have set aside for family use is a reflec-tion of greed?" I am not assuming that it does; I just want to ask my couples whether they have thought about that question.

The management system I described is the one I use, but there is no one biblical management system. Each couple must find a system that will work for them. I simply ask my couples to show me what they plan to do.

Finances are more important and time-consuming for older engaged couples, since they have had more time to form spending and saving habits, create wealth, or incur debt. I encourage you to spend more time on this subject if one or both parties bring significant resources or significant debts into the marriage. In some cases, it may be wise to ask whether a prenuptial agreement should be considered. These cases need to be handled with great care; you may want to enlist the help of your pastor for such sensitive conversations.

Chapter 7

Being a pastor has raised my awareness about the importance of the local church in the life of a newly married couple. God did not design us to live in isolation, and newly married couples would be blessed to remember that they were designed to live in a community of believers where encouragement, friendship, one-another ministry, and (sometimes) confrontation can occur. They would be blessed if they were around people who encouraged their faith, especially in a world where one's faith is often criticized or considered a sign of weakness.

In addition, it is important to teach people that they should serve. God designed each of us to function in a certain way in the body of Christ. When we function that way, several things happen: (1) We are blessed and encouraged as we watch the Lord work through us; (2) We bring honor and glory to God by being obedient to his call on our life; (3) We help Christ's body to grow by doing our part (and, when we do not function as God intended, we rob others of the ministry we were supposed to have in their lives); and (4) We serve as an example to others to function properly.

Without being legalistic, I try to emphasize that Sunday attendance, regular participation in the discipleship programs of the church, and service are nonnegotiable, because I believe that young couples (and young people in general) are helped by clear guidelines and benchmarks. My personal guideline is that couples should be participating in them forty-eight out of fifty-two weeks a year (two weeks of vacation and two weeks being sick), along with four hours of service weekly. As a mentor, you have some flexibility in how you present this, but consider this: The church is what Jesus promised to build. It is hard to argue that a person is committed to Christ without being committed to the one thing Jesus promised he would build.

My goal for this session is that the couple would have a plan to develop community during their first six months of marriage. I might ask for a longer plan if I know that they will be in the area long term.

Chapter 8

Sex is a very important topic for discussion because errors in this area create enormous hurt and consequences. Being naked with another person makes one very vulnerable, and sinful comments made at this time are rarely forgotten. I want my couples to understand that sex was designed not only for procreation but also for enjoyment. However, the enjoyment God designed is a mutual enjoyment. All substitutes like pornography and masturbation are ungodly and sinful.

In addition, since sex is designed for mutual benefit, sex is more about relationship than it is about performance. Weddings are stressful affairs and honeymoon sex, to be frank, can be a real challenge for some couples. In fact, those couples who have chosen to live as virgins to please the Lord are often the most vulnerable during the honeymoon. They have certain expectations, and sometimes those expectations are not met. It can help them to remember that, in God's economy, sex is about relationship. They can enjoy the journey of physical oneness together.

I also think it is important to help each couple see that their standard of beauty needs to change. Each culture and each individual establish a sense of beauty. That standard needs to be adjusted to reflect both the inner and the outer person of their spouse. As long as the entertainment industry sets the standard for beauty, there will be very few who can meet it, and only for so long. I want to help my couples take the first step toward freedom from the entertainment industry's tyranny.

Just as in every other area of marriage, Jesus must be the center of our sexual relationship. We have been trained (and possibly trained ourselves) to think that sex is about our enjoyment. That level of sinful selfishness can result in tremendous damage. When we remember that the gospel solved our sin problem and the ongoing provision of the Holy Spirit can help us to live godly lives, we can engage in sex for the glory of God and enjoy what God has created.

A Final Word

This book has a very simple point: Put Jesus at the center of your lives so that he will have first place in every area. As a mentor, look for as many ways as possible to make that simple point. Your mentees will not remember everything you tell them or everything found in this book, but they will remember what you stressed most. In addition to preparing your couples for decades of a strong and lasting marriage, I hope that this journey with your mentees will encourage your own spiritual growth. I find in my own counseling that I am often telling others the very things I need to hear myself. As you invest much time and energy into this material, I hope it challenges you, convicts you, and blesses you, as it has me.